The
LEADERSHIP
STAR

The
LEADERSHIP
STAR

Iftikhar Ahmed Khan

authorHOUSE®

AuthorHouse™
1663 Liberty Drive
Bloomington, IN 47403
www.authorhouse.com
Phone: 1-800-839-8640

Published by AuthorHouse   08/13/2012

ISBN: 978-1-4772-2262-1 (sc)
ISBN: 978-1-4772-2261-4 (e)

Dedicated to all those leaders who command love, respect and loyalty of their people and are willingly followed till the ends of the earth; who though are rare but their echoes prevail even after they depart.

Contents

Preface

Leadership is an enigmatic word; though talked about so frequently but understood so rarely. Almost everyone is very quick to tell the definition of leadership but tends to sink deep into meditation when asked anything beyond this traditional definition. This word has many undertones associated with it; some hear the soft bells of human element in the organization, to some it sounds like passion, energy, enthusiasm, emotions, to some it sounds like a mysterious subject, some view it like a bookish subject that doesn't work very well in practice and there are some who view it as a subject which is complicated to understand and taxing to practice.

After my initial interaction with leadership during my early months of training in Pakistan Naval Academy, I got in detailed interaction with this subject when I got posted to Navy's Human Resource Development Center. It was one fine morning when I was asked by a colleague to deliver lecture on leadership to junior officers' course as the designated instructor was away on leave. Totally bewildered but unable to refuse, I requested for an already prepared lecture which I could simply click through in lecture hall; I was provided with one and I actually clicked through with little understanding of what I said. As it would happen in any military, next time my name was already there to deliver the lecture and slowly it became a routine. After delivering the lecture 2 or 3 times, I thought of studying about theories and concepts that I usually clicked through in those lectures. As I studied this subject, I learnt that the knowledge I had was just the tip of the iceberg and much more was hidden below the surface. The more I studied, the more it looked unresolved. The pursuit to uncover the hidden aspects developed in me a craving for understanding leadership, as leadership was the life and blood of my profession. Then, a time came when I would visit sea training organization to deliver lectures on this subject to officers undergoing Command and Head of Department courses. I actually started to like this subject, and so did my audience.

With the passage of time, I developed and conducted full day workshops on leadership for officers; opportunities that helped me a lot in understanding leadership through listening to experiences of its practical manifestation. While studying the leadership literature, I came across books written by John Adair which impressed me a lot and gave me deeper insights into leadership. In fact, I found his three circles the best approach to understand functions that must be performed by a leader; this book also is heavily influenced by Adair's approach. My greatest moment came when I was invited as guest speaker to deliver a talk on leadership to faculty members and around 500 students of Pakistan Navy Engineering College. The moment was elevated further as I had my own teacher as Chief Guest, who was my teacher 20 years back when I was a sub-lieutenant undergoing training in the same institution. The mesmerizing aura of the event triggered me to transform that lecture into a book in an easy to understand language. I did it.

In this book, I have endeavored to talk about leadership in simple and free flowing language without using any complex scholastic words. I have made an effort to gather and discuss various aspects of leadership in one panorama so as to make it wholesome and meaningful. I have also tried to highlight some wrong, but common, perceptions existing about leadership and made an effort to put these perceptions right through simple arguments. Every chapter ends with keynotes to highlight important points covered in that chapter. I have also added some self-appraisal questions at the end of chapters 3-7 for readers to analyze effectiveness of their leadership in the light of this book. While developing this book primarily from my lectures, I added a flavor of field surveys to support my thoughts and ideas, results of which gave me a lot of confidence in what I have said here. It was the result of these surveys which also helped me to choose the title for this book 'The Leadership Star', because these surveys, when plotted on radar diagram, gave a five-pointer shape like a star.

This book is aimed at helping people to understand leadership, whatever field they may belong to as leadership is as essential to any field as oxygen is vital for any living thing. It is perhaps absence of true leadership that our organizations are in a constant state of drift and chaos. The only way out of this quagmire is to understand and practice leadership at all levels of an organization.

I am thankful to all those people who helped me in writing this book. Special thanks to those who responded to my surveys and provided me sincere input without which I could not have supported my thoughts. I am highly grateful to Dr Javed A Leghari, Chairman Higher Education Commission (HEC) of Pakistan, Vice Admiral (Retd) Shahid Iqbal, Rector Bahria University Pakistan and Dr Huma Haque, Humanities & Social Sciences Department, Bahria University Pakistan whose encouragement, guidance and comments helped me in making this book effective. I am extremely indebted to my worthy teachers from Preston University Karachi, Mr. Feroz Alam Khan, Mr. Raja Rab Nawaz, Mr. Zia ul Haq and Mr. Jahangir Ali Khan who are a constant source of help and guidance for me in every venture that I undertake. Last but the most important, I owe a lot to my wife and children for the comfort and convenience I received from them for working on this book. They gave a great sacrifice by allowing me to take time out from their time to work on this book. They all made me feel highly motivated to complete my work.

Iftikhar Ahmed

Chapter-1

A View Of Leadership

Leadership is one of the most discussed phenomena on earth.[1] It is the word which is most commonly used in modern day organizations but equally widely misunderstood. One cannot think of a day when one doesn't hear this word, which in fact has become a jargon in almost all walks of life; be it politics, military, bureaucracy, corporate organizations, religious or ethnic communities, educational institutions, social groups, sports teams, labor unions - you name it and the word 'Leadership' exists with its full might, albeit without full awareness as to what it really means. This existence-awareness gap results into a confusion which makes everyone practice it as per his/her own wisdom and blame '*other*' factors when failures befall them.

Though most of us agree that leadership is about moving on to the road to future by influencing and motivating people, the problem however starts beyond this academic answer when we try to explain leadership in more detail. Here are some of the misperceptions that exist about leadership:

Leadership is the job of the Head and the top management of the organization. It's these people who have the best picture and thus it's these people who must lead.

Leadership and Management are two different things; leadership determines the vision, mission and sets the objectives where as management plans, organizes and controls resources to achieve these objectives efficiently.

Leadership is the skill of dealing with human part of the organization whereas management deals with the remaining resources like machinery, infrastructure, money, information, processes, procedures etc.

Leaders are born not made; hence it is not possible to become a leader unless one has leadership attributes in his/her genes. Organizations can only groom leadership attributes lying dormant in people but cannot convert a non-leader into a leader.

Leadership is all about some qualities like initiative, courage, determination etc. If you acquire these qualities, you can become a leader.

Leadership is about learning some tips and techniques to handle people using a suitable style to be adopted in a particular situation.

These are some of many paradigms people hold about leadership in today's organizations and try to adopt an approach based on their own perception. These perceptions, with their shortcomings and flaws, have led to a situation where leadership has become almost obscured and ambiguous. Nurturing under the influence of these faulty paradigms, leaders of today have created many questions about performance and impact of leadership on organizations. This vague and bleak situation has turned into a crisis of leadership[2] where good leaders have become rare and highly sought after commodities. Despite paying astronomical salaries and choking benefits to their leaders, organizations are in a constant state of turbulence and volatility with their leaders unable to fix the situation.

This chaos has led to a situation where need for leadership is being questioned and researches are looking for alternatives to leadership i.e. substitutes for leadership. People are looking for those characteristics in Subordinate, Task and Organization that can eliminate the need for having leaders. One such approach by Kerr and Jermier is shown in Table-1.[3]

Characteristics	Impact on Leadership
Subordinate	
Experience, ability and training	Substitute for instrumental leadership
Professional orientation	Substitute for instrumental & supportive leadership
Indifference towards organization rewards	Neutralizes instrumental & supportive leadership
Task	
Structured and routine task	Substitute for instrumental leadership

Feedback within the task	Substitute for instrumental leadership
Intrinsically satisfying task	Substitute for supportive leadership
Organization	
Cohesive work groups	Substitute for instrumental & supportive leadership
Low position power of leader	Neutralizes instrumental & supportive leadership
Formalization	Substitute for instrumental leadership
Inflexibility	Neutralizes instrumental leadership
Leader physically isolated from subordinates	Neutralizes instrumental & supportive leadership

Table-1 - Kerr and Jermier Substitutes for Leadership

Let us leave the questioning of the validity of this substitutes approach towards the end of this book where I will leave it to the readers to re-visit these substitutes in the light of our discourse and conclude whether this is a valid approach or not. However, the point at this moment is why it is so that leadership has become a complex enigma which people are unable to resolve. Since we have seen and learnt about 'leadership' producing miracles, we will assume that it does work. Hence, the answer may be that there must be something wrong with our understanding of leadership which makes leadership look complex and less effective. This book will endeavor to decipher the leadership enigma in a simple manner to help people, both professionals and students, to gain an insight into leadership and get the paradigms right. However, as leadership is about humans, it therefore is as complex as humans themselves I must caution the readers here, as said by Robert Allio, (author of "The seven faces of leadership"),

> "This is not the 60-minute or 60-hour treatise that provides all you need to know about leadership in one easy reading. But for those willing to invest time and energy, I promise new insights into leadership and the leadership process".

Leadership—Personal Experience

Since our childhood, consciously or otherwise, we have been leading people and we have been led by people. At homes, parents endeavor to lead their children to the right path by constantly telling them about the good and the bad; at schools, teachers take on the responsibility of leading students to a successful life by making them educated citizens; outside homes, society leads its citizens by influencing them through its social norms, traditions and culture; at work, organizations lead people through their work environment to achieve predetermined objectives. While we come across different leaders in various stages of our lives, not all succeed in impressing us. We cherish moments spent with some while we regret those spent with others. Have you wondered, as remarked by John C Maxwell, "What makes people want to follow a leader? Why do people reluctantly comply with one leader while passionately following another to the ends of the earth?"[4]

To this question in my series of workshops and lectures on Leadership, I received as many different answers as the number of participants. Let me list down attributes which participants remembered of bad leaders so that, right at the outset, we know what makes people hate a leader:

Task-only focus, disregard for human needs/limitations

Taking people as means to achieve their own ends

Disregard for human dignity and respect

Insensitivity to work-life balance of people

Not trusting people and seeing them with suspicion

Creating an environment of fear and fright

Rude behavior with subordinates

Philosophy of punishment and deprivation

Avoiding responsibility, blaming subordinates for failures

Maintaining undue distances from people

Lacking vision, not knowing where to take the organization

Lacking courage to take risks

Curbing innovation, follow-the-book approach

Stagnation, marking time with no productivity

Too much of micro management, not allowing work freedom

Asking for output without providing resources

Having seen the traits of bad leaders, one should be able to derive attributes of good leaders by merely reversing the characteristics, however, let us hear from participants of my workshops and lectures:

Having 'human first' approach

Professional competency

Providing help and guidance to their people

Kind and compassionate

Having a caring attitude towards their people

Effective and decisive

Courageous in taking risk and accepting responsibility

Honest and fair with their people

The point being made here is that not one or few but many attributes were highlighted in the workshops to describe a successful as well as a bad leader. Another aspect that emerges from these answers is that these traits are both from 'task' and 'people' area which imply that subordinates see leadership as not only from a human perspective but task perspective as well.

What is Leadership?

The answers given above imply that leadership is much more than one can describe easily. The same dilemma emerges when we endeavor to find an all-weather definition of leadership as the existing literature offers various definitions suggested by many experts. It won't be out of place here to refer to a quote usually attributed to Dwight Eisenhower, who said:[5]

> "Leadership, I'm not sure how to define it, but I know it when I see it." (Dwight Eisenhower)

This dilemma very often surfaces when someone is asked what leadership is, this invariably results in a sudden blankness followed by sinking deep down into one's thoughts to gather the experiences and then trying to associate diverse words to express the thoughts. This is because of two extreme approaches; first, we take leaders as saviors, guardians and liberators etc, something enigmatic or mysterious which everyone cannot become, and second, we take leadership to be something so easy that it can be acquired by learning some skills, techniques and tips to apply overnight to make our people work for us. This is the way we have been conditioned by our environment.

Though many definitions of leadership exist, the one selected here for its very basic nature is of Northouse (2004), published by University of Exeter, Centre for Leadership Studies, "Leadership is a process whereby an individual influences a group of individuals to achieve a common goal."[6] Easier said than done; this '*process*' is almost like a black box, a mystery or an enigma which theorists and practitioners are constantly endeavoring to unearth and resolve to find some all-weather answer. Many theories have been put forward to describe this mysterious ability which is present in one individual and absent in the other despite the fact that everyone desires to become a good leader. However, the following definition gives us a basic framework for defining leadership:

> Leadership is a <u>process</u> whereby <u>an individual</u> <u>influences</u> a <u>group</u> of individuals to achieve a <u>common goal</u>.

An analysis of the underlined words imply that for leadership to occur, there must be a *process* in which an individual (*leader*) must have some ability to exercise influence (*authority, power*) over a group of individuals (*subordinates, followers*) to achieve a common goal (*purpose, objective, ends*). Now, these key terms in brackets are so wide-ranging that each requires a separate study to come to some understanding. However, let us not try to conclude the exact meanings of these terms here but move forward to unearth some deeper aspects of leadership, which may, in turn, help us to interpret these terms in a better way and lead us to make our own simple definition of leadership which can guide us to become effective leaders.

Leadership v/s Management Dilemma

As said earlier, the confusions existing about leadership have made it an enigma - and a very significant contribution to this confusion has been made by an unending debate over differences in leadership and management. This debate usually starts with highlighting differences between leadership and management, some of which are shown in Table-2:[7]

Leader	Manager
Innovates	Administers
Develops	Maintains
Focuses on people	Focuses on system
Inspires	Controls
Long range perspective	Short range view
Does right things	Does things right

Table-2—Leader-Manager differences

Let us have a look at what famous management gurus and experts say about differences between leadership and management:

Fred Luthans, a distinguished management professor, says that one can be a leader without being a manager and be a manager without being a leader.[8]

Stephen Covey, famous writer and author of '7 habits of highly effective people', suggests that leadership is not management; leadership has to come first and management second and further adds that management is a bottom line focus whereas leadership deals with the top line.[9]

Stephen Covey adds that management is efficiency in climbing the ladder of success; leadership determines whether the ladder is leaning against the right wall.

Warren Bennis, a famous psychologist, author and organizational consultant, says, "The manager asks how and when; the leader asks what and why."[10]

Warren Bennis adds, "Leaders conquer the context—the volatile, turbulent and ambiguous surrounding that sometimes seem to conspire against us and will surely suffocate us if we let them happen—while managers surrender to it."[11]

Ross Perot, a famous American businessman and founder of Electronic Data Systems, says, "Lead and inspire people. Don't try to manage and manipulate people. Inventories can be managed but people must be led."[12]

Peter Drucker, a famous management guru, says, "Management is doing things right; leadership is doing the right things."[13]

Robert I. Sutton, professor of management, says in his article of August 2010 in Harvard Business Review, "I am not rejecting the distinction between leadership and management, but I am saying that the best leaders do something that might properly be called a mix of leadership and management."[14]

Once, a seasoned teacher of management proudly said to me that there were about 23 differences in leadership and management. Under the influence of this environment, backed by similar literature in most management books, young graduates and managers get totally carried away by these differences between leadership and management and adapt to their self-perceived roles accordingly. During my lectures and also in general interaction and discussions with people, these differences appeared as strong dogmatic beliefs which even senior and learned people were not ready to give up. On some occasions, some senior people even got annoyed with me and refused to discuss leadership any further when I challenged this concept. A random survey done by me on managers of different sectors in lower to middle management roles also reflected this mind set. Look at some of the replies by managers to a question that what is the difference between leadership and management: (I am quoting the respondents verbatim)

> Leadership starts from one's vision to achieve something and in Management you only follow the preset procedures and policies.

> Leadership is setting vision and defining milestones, Management is achieving them.

> A leader inspires and a manager perspires.

> Management is about maintaining status quo and Leadership is about change. Leadership is about risks even when chances of failure are high. A leader says we failed while a manager says you failed.

> Management is about utilizing existing resources to their full potential and Leadership is about developing those resources much beyond their existing capabilities.

> Leadership is from the heart, while Management is from the textbook.

Leadership is all about the art of convincing others to get what you want. Management is all about how you manage operations and things, e.g. managing, controlling and organizing the work and its scenarios.

Management forces people to do something; Leadership influences people to do something where people work willingly for the sake of self-fulfillment.

Leadership is managing human beings only, while in management all resources and people are involved.

Manager's job is to plan, organize and coordinate. Leader's job is to inspire and motivate.

From these perceptions, one may be led to believe that leadership and management are two different and distinct concepts and practices. It seems that leadership deals with people and management deals with inventories and machines. The impression also emerges that leadership sits at the top and works in the broader business context with primary focus on the future whereas manager is at the lower tier, works to efficiently achieve whatever has been directed by the leader and maintains status quo. This perception gives positive undertones to leadership and negative undertones to management or in simpler words, leadership is something primary and high whereas management is something secondary and low.

This approach leads professionals in management positions to believe that they have a different job than the leaders of their organizations, they see very small role for themselves in so-called leadership functions like setting vision and defining milestones, they resort to merely following what travels down from higher ups, they simply cling to procedures & policies, they focus more on status quo and less on change, they adopt a 'things' approach and ignore humans, they become more efficiency oriented and less development oriented. Perhaps it is this compartmental approach which makes most of us believe that we are not in leadership role until we reach some higher position, and it is this flawed approach which makes the concept of leadership vague.

Though not fully justified, however, the differentiation between leadership and management is not all that bad. It does tell us what a 'Leader' does or must do. Now see the Table-2 above and read my following arguments:

If you do not know how to **administer**, your **innovation** may not be of any use, it may never be put into action to accrue the practical benefits.

If you cannot **maintain** something, there is no point in **developing** it as you will soon lose control over it and may not get the desired benefit out of it. It may actually turn into a chaos by developing in undesired directions.

Becoming **people** focused is useless if you cannot design and run a good **system**, which channelizes the skills and expertise of your people towards achievement of a common goal. An ineffective system which wastes people's skills soon leads them to demotivation which no amount of people-focus can compensate.

If you are unable to **control** and evaluate the activity for which you **inspire** your people, the failure to achieve desired results will frustrate your people and destroy their inspiration. They will not get inspired for any activity in future.

If you have the **long range perspective** but lack the skills required for a **short range view** of details, the moment you take the first step towards the long range perspective, you are pushed back by immediate hurdles which you did not foresee as you were too busy with the long range perspective. After all, every step of a ladder counts towards reaching the top of the wall.

If you do not have the skill of executing and implementing a thing in the **right way** till its completion, there is no point in determining the **right things**. Right things will soon go down the drain if not handled in a right and logical manner

Don't these arguments necessitate that leaders must have skills highlighted in the 'Manager' column else their leadership would never produce concrete results? And if you reverse the situation, won't managers, who do not have skills highlighted in the 'Leader' column, soon lead their organizations into a standstill? The natural answers to these questions would be a 'Yes'. This means leadership skills are nothing without management skills and management skills are incomplete without leadership skills. In other words, one must not put these skills into two different columns but list them under one column, named differently in different sectors i.e. 'Commander' in military, 'Manager' in corporate world, 'Supervisor' in a workplace, 'Principal' in schools, 'Captain' in sports, 'Leader' in a political party etc. However, not only misunderstood as different, the segregated concepts of leadership and management are even seen in practice in some organizations. Adapted from John Adair (2003),[15] three categories of organizations that would emerge out of this segregation paradigm would be (Fig-1):

Fig-1—Three categories of organizations

In poor organizations, leadership is seen as different from management. Resultantly, the top leadership shrinks its role to mere choosing future course, developing mission, setting objectives, making policies, issuing directives, giving decisions etc while totally alienating the managers from this process who are just supposed to implement whatever flows down from the top. The natural result of this unnatural class system is that top leadership remains ignorant of the actual state of affairs down the line and managers remain unable to understand why they are doing what they are told to do and fail to link up their work with the business strategy, leading to a gradual degeneration and ultimately demise of the organization.

In good organizations, there is a realization that top leadership, while still separate from managers, must take managers onboard in the process of setting objectives, making strategies, designing policies, sharing in decision making etc. The perception is that since managers implement the decisions, they must have some idea of the larger context. The result is that leaders get input from managers for making decisions and managers feel somewhat onboard in knowing the organization's strategy and course of action. Such an organization sails smoothly with reasonable success but never goes beyond a threshold limit and lives with routine profits.

In great organizations, business philosophy is based on forward movement for better future and the belief is that this forward momentum cannot be achieved alone by the top levels. This organization demands complete leadership role from every position, though at different levels, and expects every manager to act as a contributor towards forward movement. Hence managers are not assumed as mere administrators, maintainers, controllers, system-oriented and short-sighted but innovators, developers, people-oriented and far-sighted as well. The result is complete cohesion and harmony at all levels resulting in a synergetic movement towards greater heights. Nothing can stop such an organization from out-classing others and surging to market leadership.

Who is a Leader?

Having discussed that leadership and management are not two different concepts, let's now see who would then be into leadership role in an organization. Referring to John Adair (2005)[16], at the lowest level of an organization, the smallest group of people that work together for some specific task is called a team or a group and usually headed by a supervisor or team in-charge; this is Team Leadership level. Different tasks combine together to form one department, headed by a departmental manager having more than one Team Leaders under him/her; this is Operational Leadership level. The leader of the whole organization, having all the Operational Leaders under him/her, is the CEO or Managing Director who steers the organization as a whole; this is Strategic Leadership level. Figure-2 depicts these three levels.

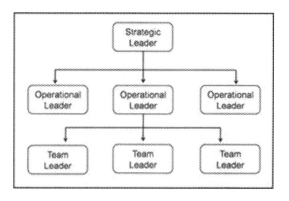

Fig-2—Three levels of leadership

Let me explain these levels a bit more by a warship example and then ask you to look at your own organization and find out these levels. The strategic leader of a warship is the Captain (Commanding Officer) who is responsible for the overall operational readiness, mission accomplishment and safety of the ship. With the input and active involvement of his subordinates, he sets the overall ship's objectives, makes a long term strategy to achieve these objectives and continuously monitors the progress towards achievement of these objectives. He is normally assisted by four officers who head Operations, Mechanical Engineering, Weapons Engineering and Logistics departments. These are called Heads of Departments (HODs) and are the Operational Leaders of the ship. They draw their own departmental objectives from Ship's overall objectives, make a strategy for achieving these objectives, arrange resources, train and develop their personnel to undertake department's operational and administrative tasks and coordinate and plan day to day activities. These HODs have different teams working under them. For example, the teams working under Operations HOD (who is also called the Executive Officer and is the Second-in-Command of the ship) are Navigation Team, Communications Team, Warfare Team, Seamanship Team, Safety Team and Welfare Team which are headed by respective specialists who work as Team Leaders. These Team Leaders draw their team objectives from the Operations Department objectives and ensure that their people are trained and ready to undertake relevant tasks as required. That's how the ship's overall objectives are converted into departmental objectives and then down to team objectives and to day to day tasks. Every level is headed by officers having different designations but all are leaders for their part of the ship, each is responsible not only to plan for today but look for future as well and each is required to maintain team comradeship and look after the welfare of his people.

The discussion here is aimed at concluding that organizations require leaders at not one but all levels.

Therefore, the impression that leaders exist only at the top and leadership is different from management may not be true and needs to be replaced by the reality that unless leadership exists at all levels, an organization cannot move forward to achieve its vision and mission. Hence, when it comes to the question as to who is the leader in an organization, the answer lies in the fact that there are many leaders in an organization working at different levels each contributing towards achievement of organizational goals translated to various activities at his/her level. Let us close this discussion here with a quote from John Adair, "In today's turbulent world, effective leadership at every level of an organization is essential."

Before moving on to the next chapter on theoretical perspectives, let us have a look at some keynotes to remember from this chapter.

Keynotes

Here are some important keynotes to remember:

- Leadership is the word which is most commonly used in modern day organizations but equally widely misunderstood. This existence-awareness gap results into a confusion which makes everyone practice leadership as per his/her own wisdom.

- Many wrong perceptions and paradigms exist about leadership. Living with these perceptions, leaders of today have created many questions about performance and impact of leadership on organizations, which has led to a situation where need for leadership is being questioned and researches are looking for substitutes to leadership.

- A very significant contribution to this misunderstanding has been made by the debate over differences between leadership and management. Many experts see leadership and management as two different concepts. Not only misunderstood as different, leadership and management are even practiced as two different concepts in most organizations which is the major cause of organizational failure.

- Leadership and management are not two different concepts but different names for one concept; the name depends upon the field in which it is practiced i.e. 'Commander' in military, 'Manager' in corporate world, 'Supervisor' in a workplace,

'Principal' in schools, 'Captain' in sports, 'Leader' in a political party etc.

- The impression that leaders exist only at the top and leadership is different from management may not be true and need to be replaced by the realities that unless leadership exists at all levels, an organization cannot move forward to achieve its vision and mission.

- Great organizations take leadership and management not as two different but same concepts. These organizations demand and facilitate complete leadership role from every position at different levels.

- In an organization, the three levels of leadership, as suggested by John Adair, are: Team Leadership at the lowest level of an organization, Operational Leadership at the level where different teams join together to form a department and Strategic Leadership where all departments join to form one organization.

Chapter-2

The Theoretical Perspective

Having discussed what leadership is and who is a leader in an organization, the natural quest would be to learn how to become a leader. Such questions usually lead people to study existing theories, try to relate these theories with current practices and endeavour to learn to become effective in that very field. Following this natural course, let us examine theories of leadership. However, a word of caution here - leadership is as old as the mankind itself and it is as complex as the humanity itself, resultantly, one may come across an enormous amount of research leading to many leadership theories emerging out of this research. Since the aim is not to overburden ourselves, therefore we will restrict ourselves to some important theories which turned the course of leadership practice. Let's start with the earliest existing theory about leadership i.e. Trait Theory.

Traits Approach

Leadership, in its earliest form, was centered on personalities called 'Great Men', and hence the 'Great Man Theory'. Given today's knowledge about leadership, this theory was primarily focused on 'Leader'.

The spirit of this theory was that leaders are born, not made. This theory assumed that there are some persons who are born great with super human qualities and who will always find their way to leadership roles. These qualities, like physical appearance, muscularity, physical courage, impressive voice, tall height etc were considered to be the hallmarks of great men. This theory gave rise to super human heroes who would appear in times of great need and save their men from desolation. Carlyle's heroes, Nietzsche's great blond beast, Hegel's evoker and carrier of the spirit of the times, Sidney Hook's event-making man etc show the exact essence of this theory.[17] With the passage of time and watching closely those who were successful leaders, some more personal traits were identified like intelligence, determination, initiative, honesty, integrity, loyalty etc and the 'Great Man Theory' took the name of 'Trait Theory'. However, still leadership was restricted to some qualities and the underlying essence was that some men, and not all, can have these qualities. Though this theory enabled researchers to study men / women at the top of an organization but the prime limitation of this approach was that a researcher could not use this theory to analyze the contributions of followers.[18]

Though the Trait Theory tries to explain leadership, this approach offers a diverse list of traits that were supposed to be present in leaders. No two lists would appear same either in type or number of traits. Peter G. Northouse has shown lists of leadership traits concluded by different studies of leadership traits and character, these are: Stogdill (1948) 8 traits, Mann (1959) 6 traits, Stogdill (1974) 10 traits, Lord DeVader and Alliger (1986) 3 traits, Kirkpatrick and Locke (1991) 6 traits and Zaccaro, Kemp and Bader (2004) 11 traits.[19] US Army lists down 23 traits of character of a good leader.[20] John C. Maxwell has listed 21 qualities in his famous book 'The 21 Indispensable Qualities of a Leader'.[21]

Following this approach, teaching of leadership focused on highlighting leadership qualities to the audience, accompanied with emotional quotes from scholars and professionals. Such sessions began with an ambiguity about leadership, ended with a conviction that one can be a leader only if one has these qualities and gave nothing to the participants to practice leadership after leaving the training halls. It reminds me of my Commanding Officer at the Navy's HR Development Center who narrated an incidence when he was a young Commander and was given a lecture on leadership by a seasoned Admiral, "It was the same old sermon on qualities; be sincere, be loyal, be honest, have high integrity, have courage, have determination etc. At the end of Q&A session, totally bewildered, I raised my hand and was given a warm welcome by the speaker to ask question. I stood up and asked not for 'freedom of speech' but for 'freedom after speech'. When graciously granted, I asked that the qualities which the speaker had talked about could only be practiced by Hazrat Moosa—(Prophet Moses, PBUH) and not by us, so would the respectable speaker tell us what we should do as normal human beings to practice leadership from tomorrow?" (I leave it to common sense of readers to imagine the probable response of the worthy speaker and the fate of 'freedom after speech'.)

This approach to teaching leadership is practiced even today. One often finds courses on leadership titled "Leadership Qualities" which primarily focus on those desired traits which a leader 'must' acquire without telling 'how' to acquire. To quote from my own experience, I was invited by a renowned organization as a guest speaker to deliver a lecture on the topic "Leadership Qualities" as this very title was part of their approved training programme. I had to really convince the management to change the topic to "Leadership" to make it more comprehensive and meaningful. A typical problem with qualities approach is that qualities or traits that one book or course delineates are usually different from the other. This is what the dilemma of qualities approach is. We not only don't know what common qualities of good leaders are, we also don't know how to train people to become honest, determined, enthusiastic, loyal, courageous etc except giving them emotional sermons. It is actually up to the people whether they choose or don't choose to be honest, determined, enthusiastic, loyal and courageous.

Though qualities have tremendous impact on leadership but qualities alone are not enough to become a leader. Qualities approach tells us some vital traits without which leaders may not be very effective i.e. we can hardly imagine a good leader who is not honest, not determined to achieve his/her goals, lacks enthusiasm, lacks persistence, is un loyal to his/her people and has no courage to take risks or accept responsibility. Look around and you will see that almost all renowned leaders in all the fields had or have these traits to reach the top.

Situational Approach

Though qualities approach endeavored to determine qualities of leaders, however, there were many problems intrinsic to this approach. These limitations of qualities approach turned the focus of researchers from 'Leader' to studying the 'Situation' in which leadership was happening[22].

Proponents of this approach professed that in a given situation, the person having the required set of qualities will emerge as a leader. They added that a person having certain qualities and was very effective in one situation may not be that effective in another. Frequently quoted example to support this argument was Winston Churchill, who was a heroic leader as Prime Minister of Britain during World War II but failed to retain his effectiveness in post-war years.[23] Research on 'Situation' led to conclusions that qualities required for becoming an effective leader in one situation might not be very helpful if the situation changed. This theory argues that leaders must have knowledge and skills required by the situation and must know how to apply this knowledge and skill with reference to a particular situation.

The requirement of desired competence, and the skill to apply this competence with reference to a particular situation, led to studies on leadership styles. The outcome of this initiative was different models recommending suitable style to be adopted by leaders in different situations. Most popular of these models are of Blake & Mouton, Fred Fiedler and Blanchard & Hersey.[24] These studies focused on various factors that influence leadership like task, relationship, follower's competence and motivation, leader's position power etc. These studies, in general, suggest that there is no one universal style that ought to be adopted in every situation but style must change as does the situation. Different leadership styles that emerge from these studies, based on the situations in which leadership operates, are autocratic, democratic, free reign, task-oriented, human-oriented, directive, supportive, delegative etc. These studies leave it to the person in leadership role to select the style best suited to the situation (*discussed in Leadership Style part*).

Though situational approach takes the focus away from leader and endeavors to look into the situational variables, it focuses merely on the way a leader should handle subordinates rather than talking about those deeply embedded vital functions that leaders are required to perform in a group. In other words, this approach still looks more at 'leader' and less at the 'group' of subordinates who contribute immensely towards accomplishment of organizational objectives and tasks.

Like the qualities approach, Leadership Styles also attracted management trainers and was made part of teaching/training curriculum. Unlike qualities, 'Styles' were received with enthusiasm as these could be learnt and adopted quickly. However, this approach has been taken by some managers more as 'tips and techniques' of leadership which provide a quick fix approach to becoming effective leaders overnight. Once during my workshop on leadership, I observed a young stylish manager getting uncomfortable when I started to talk about understanding of humans for effective leadership. Soon he raised his hand and asked as to when I would be talking about those things which he could quickly note down to lead his people. I replied that it would not be possible for me without talking about humans first as understanding humans and their needs is very important for leaders. This reply, however, could not put him at ease and as I expected, he did not return to the workshop after tea break. Leadership 'styles' is still a hot topic in leadership training today. Managers are enthusiastic to know whether they should be autocratic, democratic, directive, delegative, supportive or free reign. However, despite following the recommended style, they frequently struggle with leadership problems in their organizations, reaching the conclusion that either leadership courses do not work or leadership skills come by birth and not by training.

Despite its shortcomings, Situational Approach is not all that inconclusive; it provides us an insight that there is no one universal style which leaders have to stick to in order to lead their people rather they must adopt style suitable to the situation. It is specially an eye opener for those people in leadership positions who tend to handle their people throughout with one typical style of leadership. One may come across many senior people who carry tainted paradigms about leadership style and believe that subordinates always require strict direction and control to make them work and that carrot and stick style works the best. However, they do not know that sticking on to such a style in every situation may lead to 'Movement' and not 'Motivation', as asserted by Fredrick Herzberg in his Hygiene Theory of Motivation.[25]

On the contrary, one may also come across people who adopt a free reign style in every situation; an approach which they assume would be welcomed by subordinates but which actually makes the task suffer, leading to despair of subordinates and degeneration of the organization.

The trait approach and situational approach together contributed towards discovering some secrets of the leadership enigma and helped people in learning to become effective leaders. However, the complex group dimensions, human interactions and needs that form the major part of leadership, still remained undiscovered lying below the surface.

Group Approach

The shortcomings of Trait and Situational Approaches led to shifting of focus towards the third vital element of leadership system i.e. the group.

The group approach has its roots in social psychology. This approach takes leadership as an exchange process between the leader and the followers. It professes that there must be a positive exchange between the leader and followers in order for group goals to be accomplished. The 'exchange' in this approach is the investment done by each side for each other to get something in return. This investment can be anything leading to achievement of common purpose.[26]

Within this exchange relationship between the leader and followers, group approach looks at those functions which a leader performs within in the group. Various management (and also Leadership) functions in an organization, given in management books are Planning, Communicating, Organizing, Staffing, Leading, Coordinating, Controlling and Rewarding. Functions are those activities which a leader must perform to achieve the objective. Without performing the functions, an objective can never be achieved, whatever may be the style that the leader adopts and whatever qualities he/she may have. For example, a mother besides being kind, loving, compassionate and gracious towards her child, must also sacrifice her own rest and sleep to feed the child, to keep the child clean and protect the child as these are vital functions which must be performed at all costs if the child is to survive. Similarly, a gardener has to work under the harshness of weather to nurture the plant for it to grow, besides being concerned, caring and devoted towards it, as whatever may be the level of concern and devotion, the plant will soon die if not nurtured. Such is the importance of vital functions that a leader has to perform.

John Adair has provided a very comprehensive view of three areas of group needs that must be fulfilled by a leader. These are Task needs, Team needs and Individual needs. Adair shows their relationship in form of three interacting circles. (Fig-3)[27]

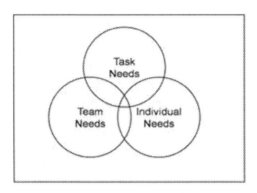

Fig-3—Group needs by John Adair

Adair highlights that these are the three main functional areas where leaders have to perform. According to Adair, these three circles interact with each other; any accomplishment in one circle will boost the other two and any failure in one circle will jeopardize the working of the other two. Quite often in our professional lives we observe that a leader who focuses too much on task, becomes a hard-task master and ignores the needs of his/her subordinates, usually leads to frustration among subordinates and eventually disappearing of team spirit in the organization which in turn has devastating impact on achievement of the task as well. On the other hand, we also see that a leader, who fails to build up the team spirit, leads to an environment of individualism where people take their colleagues as competitors not comrades and as barriers in the way of getting rewards. Such an atmosphere leads to internal politics and eventually results in lack of synergy which ultimately makes the task suffer. And we may also come across a leader who focuses too much on happiness of people at the cost of the task. In such an organization, failure in achievement of task not only gradually leads to individual frustration but also breaking up of the team cohesion.

Functional approach completely eliminates the philosophy that leaders are born not made, as performance of these functions does not require genes but learning, common sense and logic. This approach has now become the foundation for leadership training. It is based on learning sessions about various areas where leadership must focus and vital tasks that leader must perform. However, as with other two approaches, problems may appear in this approach as well if functions are seen in isolation. A strict focus on functions and even successful execution of these may sometimes not accrue the desired results. Though professional competence may lead to success in task area, however, maintaining the team and managing the individuals would certainly require backing up by sound personal traits of the leader and selecting leadership style suitable to the situation.

Towards a Holistic Approach

Though the research on leadership is ever growing and many theories have been put forward, the three approaches discussed above provide a general theoretical roadmap of leadership studies. Having discussed the said three approaches, one can easily come to a conclusion that no single approach is wholesome and each has some shortcomings. Shortcomings notwithstanding, each approach does provide an insight into the leadership system which helps us in taking a step forward. This step forward must make use of all the three approaches and combine findings of all of these into one single model which though may not be ultimate but useful in seeing the complete panorama of leadership. With this intention, let us see what the holistic approach to leadership would look like.

The holistic approach must combine the findings of all the three approaches and endeavor to see leadership as a whole. Let us re-visit every approach and see what it has got to contribute towards a holistic approach.

Traits Approach - There are some <u>qualities</u> which help people in becoming effective leaders.

Situational Approach—Leadership <u>style</u> must be selected based on the situation in which the group is working.

Group Approach—Leaders are required to perform certain generic <u>functions</u> in a work group.

This brief re-cap helps us in determining the three vital characteristics of a leader i.e. Qualities, Style and Functions. As said earlier, none of these characteristics alone can fully explain the concept of leadership but if seen together, they lead us to an understanding of the complete panorama. Let us understand these characteristic by a simple explanation:

'Qualities' show what you are as a leader

'Style' shows how you deal with others as a leader

'Functions' tell what you do as a leader

As one can see here, these elements are not mutually exclusive but complementary to each other. This can be supported with following arguments:

You perform your functions very well but you do not know how to handle your subordinates in a given situation, chances are that your 'Functions' will not bring desired results.

You are a weather-vane and know very well how to handle your subordinates in different situations but you cannot deliver the basic functions required of you, you will surely fail to achieve the desired objectives.

You perform your functions very well and also know how to handle your subordinates in different situations but lack those vital traits which bring you closer to the hearts of your subordinates, chances are that your achievements become short-lived and you lack wholehearted support of your subordinates.

Survey Support for Holistic Approach

Having seen that one cannot be a good leader without excelling in the three basic areas of Qualities, Style and Functions, and breaking down the 'Functions' into three sub-areas i.e. Task, Team, Individual, as discussed with reference to John Adair, we can get five fundamental elements i.e. Qualities, Style, 'Task, Team and Individual'.

In order to see the relative importance of these five theoretical elements in successful leadership, I conducted a random survey which was aimed at seeing as to how people described their most beloved leader. This was not a classical research but was a general survey to ascertain the feelings of respondents in describing their beloved leader.

The survey was based on 16 statements encompassing these five elements, and was randomly administered to 150 persons in lower to middle management levels in different sectors. The participants were asked to think of the leader who impressed them most in their careers and with whom they worked wholeheartedly, and would love to work again, and then rate the leader's attributes on the Likert Scale 1-5 (1—very weak, 2—weak, 3—moderate, 4—strong, 5—very strong). The data was analyzed and the mean of the ratings given to five elements was transformed to a radar diagram (Fig-4). The dark line in the figure connects points, on each element, plotted for survey replies.

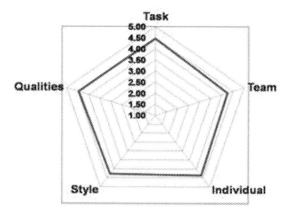

Fig-4—Radar diagram

If you see the figure, the mean of the ratings on all five elements falls between 3.5 and 4.5, which shows that the participants were impressed by the leader who had all of these five elements with good intensity. This supports my assertion that one cannot be a good leader without excelling in all the five basic areas of Qualities, Style, Task, Team and

Individual. This also implies that these five elements are not options but compulsions and that the basic mother-theories from which these elements emerge must be seen in one big perspective. The conclusion, therefore, is that unless a leader gives due focus to task, endeavors to build and maintain the team, takes care of his/her people, adopts the right leadership style and has sound qualities, he/she cannot become an effective leader and will seldom command respect and love of his/her people.

The Leadership Star

From this radar diagram, I took the five corners and joined them with the center, which resulted into a star. Look at the picture in Fig-5:

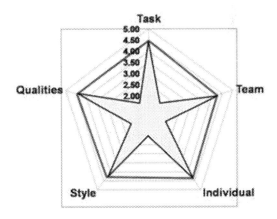

Fig-5—Radar with Star

And if I remove the radar diagram and further refine the picture, we get a perfect nice star (Fig-6), which I call

'The Leadership Star', which became the title of this book and format of the remaining part of the text.

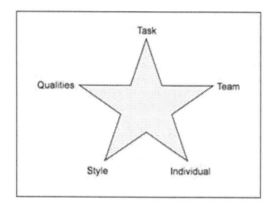

Fig-6—Leadership Star

Let us move on and discuss, as separate chapters, these five points of the Leadership Star one by one in the sequence Task, Team, Individual, Style and Qualities; this being a sequence in which, I feel, these aspects are more readily visible to an observer. Before we move to the next chapter, let me list down some keynotes for you to remember from this chapter.

Keynotes

Here are some important keynotes to remember:

- Leadership, in its earliest form, was centered on personalities called 'Great Men' and advocated that some qualities lead people into leadership role. Later this theory took the name of 'Trait Theory'. This approach offers a diverse list of traits that must be present in leaders; however, no two lists appear completely same either in type or number of traits.

- Situational Approach professed that in a given situation, the person having the required set of qualities will emerge as a leader. This theory highlights that leaders must have knowledge and skills required by the situation at hand. Different leadership styles that emerge from studies are autocratic, democratic, free reign, task-oriented, human-oriented, directive, supportive, delegative etc.

- The Group Approach looks at those functions which a leader must perform within in the group to achieve the objective. John Adair's three interacting areas for leaders to perform functions are task, team and individual; success in one area boosts the other two and failure in one area jeopardizes the other two.

- No single approach is wholesome and each has some shortcomings. The holistic approach must combine the findings of all the three approaches and endeavor to see leadership as a whole. The five essential elements must be Qualities, Style, Task, Team and Individual. Leaders must give equal focus to all these five elements.

Chapter-3

Performing The Task

Importance of Task

Task is the very reason for which people come and work together. It is the task which becomes the basis for compensation and benefits. In fact, an organization, by definition, is an entity comprising people who work together to achieve a common task. Success or failure in task has direct impact on an organization's success and naturally has a direct impact on its people. Hence it is the task which is the most important factor in any team or organization. One may come across organizations where the leadership (or the management) fails to give the right focus to task which leads to breeding of an environment of politics, mistrust and blame-game. One, who has work experience, would support the fact that failure in achieving the task frustrates people and ultimately leads to breaking up of the team as well.

Leaders must understand that the prime function for which they have been put into leadership role is the achievement of the task. It is the success or failure in the tasks that determines success or failure of a leader. No one would honor a leader who failed in achieving the task though being a good team player and compassionate to his/her people. In fact, failure in task would lead to frustrating the team and creating frustration among individuals no matter how much care was given to the team and people by the leader.

Task Functions of a Leader

The tasks and functions given in various management books that leaders have to accomplish are Planning, Communicating, Organizing, Staffing, Leading, Coordinating, Evaluating, Controlling and Rewarding etc. Before we move any further, let me ask here that aren't these functions of Managers as we study in management books? I am sure that you will say 'Yes'. Well, since these functions are talked about in management books, it is mostly from here that we see these functions as those of Managers and not Leaders, and see management as a different concept from leadership. While reserving these functions for Managers, we tend to believe that Leaders do something different from these. We then justify our perceptions with arguments that Leaders work beyond these functions and primarily determine the overall direction, set the strategic vision and motivate people to work wholeheartedly to pursue this vision. It is from this paradigm that we see leadership different from management. You will agree with me that these functions are supposed to be performed by anyone given responsibility of a team, department or the organization and may be called a Supervisor, Manager, Commander, Principal, Captain, Director etc. If that is true then where is that 'Leader' who does not perform these functions in an organization and merely sticks to determining the overall direction, setting the strategic vision and motivating people? Such a 'Leader' then has very limited role to play and, in fact, may not be required at all. In my view, such a leader does not exist anywhere. Leadership is not different from management; it simply adopts a different name in different sectors. These functions have to be performed by any one heading any organizations. As you move on, you will tend to agree more with me. Let us take some important functions of leaders or managers for discussion albeit without going into much detail as these functions are very elaborately covered in management books (Fig-7).

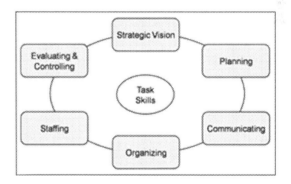

Fig-7—Task Skills

Strategic Vision

Alice, in Wonderland, asked the cat, "Would you please tell me which way to go from here?" The cat replied, "That depends upon where you want to get to." Such is the importance of knowing where one wants to get to before planning other details of the journey because a lot depends upon answering this question. This, in organizational terms, is called Vision which tells where an organization wants to be in future.

Strategic vision guides an organization where to invest and where not to venture. We may come across organizations where many things seem to happen like new acquisitions, new systems, new structures, new product lines, new marketing strategies, new HR standards, new policies etc, but one cannot see a linkage between them as they do not flow out of the strategic vision but result from isolated decisions. Though a lot of activity seems to be taking place but such organizations ultimately remain stagnant and waste their precious resources in unwanted directions.

A strong and compelling vision not only sets the future destination but also energizes people towards this future and helps in setting objectives that move the organization step by step to this destination. This means that a clear strategic vision provides the starting point for organizational alignments; alignment between vision and mission, mission and objectives, objectives and strategy, strategy and plans etc. I had an opportunity to visit an organization that had set a vision "Our passion is to attain a position of leadership among success stories of tomorrow." I asked the top management whether they ensured that their mission and yearly objectives were set in line with this vision. The reply was that it was an intangible thing and couldn't be converted to objectives. I further inquired as to how they knew whether they were moving ahead on this road. The reply I got was that it was an intangible thing and couldn't be known. I didn't give up and inquired as to whether their lower employees knew what the vision of the organization was. The answer was a big proud 'Yes'. Then I asked whether the employees knew as to how they were contributing to this over all vision. The answer was "It's an intangible thing". I gave up and surrendered; and concluded a label for this vision, 'Vision Intangible'. Such a vision is merely an emotional slogan and has no guidance value.

Vision has a central place in leadership; it leads the leader. It is like a candle in the darkness which becomes a source of guidance and keeps helping us in moving on the right path. Like, without a candle in darkness, we tend to go arbitrarily here and there, similarly without vision there is no progress forward but hops and jumps here and there. Strategic vision distinguishes good leaders from bad leaders. Good leaders continuously keep their future in sight and adopt the right course to be steered well before the organization ends up in a quagmire, as a famous quote says:

> "A good Captain is on the lookout for shifting trends, changing needs, storms and icebergs while bad ones are deeply stuck up with today."

Leaders must set a strategic vision which should tell people where the organization wants to be in future. A clear vision helps people to determine the route to destination, especially in highly volatile situations when things change at a great speed, even when no clear policies or guidelines exist. In the absence of a clear vision, organization and its people do not know as to where they are heading for, and when this awareness doesn't exist, they cannot set their sails to shape course to their desired destination, as said by Lucius Annaeus Seneca, a Roman philosopher and statesman (1 BC-65 AD):

"When a man does not know what harbor he is making for, no wind is the right wind."

Since vision determines the future destination, energizes people towards this future, helps in setting objectives and provides a starting point for organizational alignments, it must therefore be set with a lot of prudence. Some broad aspects in setting vision are discussed below.

Have Knowledge   Vision must never be a 'talk in the air' else it will go in the air and fail to accrue its true benefits. A meaningful vision comes only through sound knowledge. Setting of a strategic vision requires not only job knowledge but also the bigger picture. This bigger picture comes from job knowledge, organizational knowledge, industry knowledge and environmental (political, economic, social and technological) knowledge. Without a comprehensive view of all these aspects, leaders may end with very high chances of miscalculations and failures. For example, a vision that envisages the 'Best' or 'Number-1' state for an organization would be meaningless if it has been set without the organizational, industry and environmental knowledge. Hence, for determining vision for an organization, its leaders must ensure that they have the right kind of knowledge else the result will be less a Vision and more a castle in the sky.

Envision the Best State   A vision that aims for ordinary future state, receives ordinary response. Hence, the vision must exhibit the best possible state for the organization. Also, remember that people get more motivated by future that provides 'them' with the best state of existence. This implies, along with the best state for the organization, the vision must show the best state for its people as well. I came across an organization which had set its vision as, "To be a Rs. 50 billion company by 2030." Now, though this Vision sets a tangible future state of the organization, it has strong overtones of wellbeing of its owners and weaker shades for best state of its people. Such Visions may not trigger motivation of the people and, hence, may not get translated into whole-hearted participation by them. If leaders care for well-being of their people, they must make it explicit and integrate this philosophy into every stage of their strategic thought process.

Maintain Fantasy-Pragmatism Balance   It is good to have fantasies but fantasies alone don't earn living for anyone. There must be a rational blend of fantasies and pragmatism in one's life else it is more of daydreaming and less of practical life. So is the case with organizations. Envisioning the best state does not mean a fantasy of taking the organization to moon rather a future which though may not be fully achievable yet motivating for people to keep working with willingness, enthusiasm and eagerness to reach it. Remember that there is a difference between a Vision and a Fantasy; for a person, there can be a 'vision' to achieve the highest qualification in his/her specific field but it will be 'fantasy' to think of becoming master of all the fields in his/her lifetime. Similarly, a local shoe company, with limited resources, facing world-class shoe stores can have a 'vision' to offset the opponents in local market with suitable strategy but it will be a 'fantasy' if it aims for market leadership across the globe. Such a fantasy will be seen as non-serious by its people and become demotivating instead of triggering enthusiasm. Since strategic vision must become a source of guidance for an organization, it must therefore be less a fantasy and more an upward-looking pragmatic vision which can help the organization in determining its mission, objectives, strategy and tactics/plans.

Maintain Customer Focus Can you name any organization which says it doesn't have customers? All organizations have customers, though seen differently in different sectors. It is not the management or the people of an organization who determine its success rather it is the customers who have the veto power. If customers don't see any value for them in an organization, why would they come to this organization or use its products? Coming again to the vision, "To be a Rs. 50 billion company by 2030", what do you, as a customer, see for yourself in this vision? You will perhaps feel only as a contributor to the wealth of the organization—its owners, its management and its employees, right? You will, most likely, be attracted by another company whose vision speaks of care and concern for you, not expansion of their own wealth. This is why it is important to maintain customer focus in vision statement. And this is why most of the successful organizations have in their visions phrases like 'care for customers', 'value for customers', 'quality for customers' etc. This also helps an organization's own people to think of customers and keep customers in focus all the time, and this focus, if maintained, gets translated into customer-oriented performance.

Planning

A plan provides a bridge between today and tomorrow. Some organizations spend a lot of time and valuable resources in planning, loads of input and suggestions are taken from everywhere and files are moved from office to office only to end up in doing more and more planning with no concrete plan coming out. We must never forget that it is not the planning but the result of this planning i.e. the Plan, which helps us in moving forward. Leaders must ensure that there is a plan to move forward towards the strategic vision. Making a plan involves setting of objectives, making a strategy and arranging resources to achieve these objectives.

Objectives As said earlier, vision looks into broader and farther future state. In organizational context, this vision must be converted into mission, which states as to what the organization does to achieve its vision. Mission therefore is an effort to put into tangible terms the direction for the organization to move onto the road to its desired future destination. Still, however, this mission cannot be purposely achieved unless the organization knows what effects it must generate to achieve it. These effects are called the objectives. Hence, the vision or mission must not be left as only slogans on the walls but must be converted into objectives on long-term as well as short-term basis. This means, objectives must flow out of organization's vision and mission else neither vision nor objectives will have any meaningfulness for the organization and its people. If an organization envisions expanding eastwards but its objectives pull it westwards, this divergent pursuit will not only waste valuable resources but also result in failure in both directions. Objectives must be set at all levels and must be aligned i.e. higher objectives guiding lower. Objectives must never be vague statements but these must be SMART (Specific, Measurable, Agreeable, Realistic, Time-bound). However, these factors must change their focus according to the focus of the level of objectives with a funnel down approach; more strategic and broad objectives at the top, more tactical and specific objectives as we move down. Don't be unrealistic to ask your people to bring stars from heavens. Unrealistic and vague objectives not only lead to frustration and demotivation but also do not help in evaluation and control. I came across a very experienced person who worked for a nautical company with good salary package but left to take up a less paid job. When asked why he decided to quit, he replied that the previous company had set objectives for him that he could never achieve even if he gave his life and blood, so instead of living every day with frustration and dejection, he preferred to quit and work elsewhere. Let me quote another example to show as to how vague objectives demotivate a person. I know a professor who, after retirement from university teaching, was hired by a consulting firm at a handsome package to be a part of their think-tank. However, several months after joining, the firm could not give any clear tasks/objectives to him. Upon many requests to tell him what to do, he was told that his presence in the think-tank was of strategic importance for them. The result; the professor left the firm within a year as he could not find any meaningfulness in the organization.

Strategy Strategy has its origins in military. It is the overall plan of the general to employ his forces to beat his enemy and reach the military objectives. This takes into account factors like overall politico-military environment, factors affecting achievement of the aim, strengths and weaknesses of enemy forces, own strengths and weaknesses, hypotheses of enemy courses of action, own courses of action, employment plan, execution, logistics, command and control etc. Importance of strategy has long been recognized by the world outside military. Strategy is the plan of an organization to move from where it is today to where it wants to be tomorrow while facing challenges, competitions, threats, risks etc. Unless there is a strategy, there is no direction. Without a sound strategy, an organization is continuously beaten by the external as well as internal factors. It becomes like a kite with broken thread which is on the mercy of wind and goes wherever wind takes it. Strategy must take into account the external and internal environments, threats and opportunities, own strengths & weaknesses and resources at hand. The strategic process must result into various courses of action available and selection of the best course of action along with a plan to follow this course to achieve own objectives. This strategic direction should then guide all other actions like departmental plans, equipment inductions, processes, procedures, campaigns etc. Organizations without a long term strategy can be instantly identified by frequently changing policies, random and unrelated system inductions, unexpected process changes, sudden efficiency campaigns etc. Such organizations get a totally different direction with the change of top leadership; with every newcomer doing new experiments. For organizations to succeed, there must be a long term strategy to go where they want to go, and which must not change with the new leadership coming in, unless there is a significant change in environment which necessitates reviewing the strategy. Once the strategy is finalized, leaders must ensure that all the required efforts and resources are put into it to achieve the desired ends. Strategy must then guide the development and selection of tactics which are the specific day-to-day maneuvers undertaken to achieve strategic ends. For example, strategy of winding up from one market to penetrate forcefully in the other to offset the competition must be converted into tactics for efficient withdrawal from one market and intelligent infiltration in the other. Since strategic competition has almost taken the shape of corporate wars, organizations have a lot to learn from military tactics[28]. Military concepts like Center of Gravity, Decisive Points, Critical Vulnerabilities, Counter-attack, Counter-offensive, Riposte, Defensive balance force and Strategic reserves all can be applied to business wars in the market. Phillip Kotler (2003) in his book *Marketing Management* has mentioned that given clear opponent and objectives, five military attack strategies are available; these are Frontal attack, Flank attack, Encirclement attack, Bypass attack and Guerrilla warfare that can be employed in businesses.[29]. These attack tactics can very well be applied in business to out-maneuver the opponent by attacking his product or strong areas with smarter moves suitable to the situation.

Resources Money makes the mare go, so do the resources which provide means to achieve strategy ends. Don't go overboard in setting strategies which do not match your resources, keep in mind what Field Marshal Montgomery highlighted as the first rule of strategy, "The Commander-in-Chief must be sure that what is strategically desirable is technically possible with the resources at his disposal." More often, the underlying reason for failure, frustration and demotivation in organizations is non-availability of resources compatible with the task.

And don't forget, 'resources' not only mean men, money, machines and tools but also information, required time and supportive environment. Though 'scarcity of resources' is a valid paradigm and organizations must learn to live with this reality, however, it is the artificially created scarcity which hurts organizations the most. Such artificial scarcity is very widely seen in many organizations that suddenly wake up from snooze of prolonged mismanagement and misuse of resources and take abrupt measures to plug the resource hemorrhage, even starving the vital projects. The undue downsizing, intentional understaffing, irrational saving campaigns and unreasonable urgency paradigms etc are some indicators of such a state that hurts more than the real scarcity paradigm. Sleeping over an issue, for example ignoring maintenance of a machine which is causing significant specification variations for the last three years, and suddenly awakening and asking your subordinates to prepare an immediate report, without giving them enough time, funds and required input by experts, is one such example of artificial scarcity of resources which damages organizations. Leaders must identify resources and then provide these resources to people to perform the task. Remember that each and every thing in required resources is relevant and important. Do you know that a horseshoe nail was responsible for loss of a kingdom? If not, then read this proverb, "For want of a nail, the horseshoe was lost; for want of a horseshoe, the horse was lost; for want of a horse, the rider was lost; for want of a rider, the battle was lost; for want of a battle, the kingdom was lost and all for the want of a horseshoe nail."[30] Isn't it an eye opener for those leaders who keep their people resource-starved in undue pursuit of saving resources?

Communicating

Communication is the lifeblood of an organization. As the blood provides oxygen and vital food components to all parts of a body, effective communication provides vital information from one level to the other and from one corner to the other of an organization. Absence of communication creates vacuum which invites rumours. For communication to become effective, leaders must ensure following aspects:

Supportive Environment Communication must become the most sought after activity in the organization and people must feel free to communicate. Many innovative ideas are killed either due to absence of communication or due to fear of negative backlash. Leaders must learn to 'listen' not 'hear' and must also inculcate this habit in their people. This listening does not come merely by so called 'Open door' policies but by interacting with people informally and dropping down to their level to understand their language. I have experienced that when you frequently sit with your people at their own places and get involved in their activities, they tend to open up their hearts and minds and give you their sincere input. Nothing better can explain such an environment than famous epistle of Hazrat Ali (May Allah be pleased with him), a prominent companion of Prophet Muhammad (Peace be upon him) and the fourth caliph of Islam, when he directed Malik Ashtar, Governor of Egypt:

> "Meet the oppressed and the lowly periodically in an open conference, and be conscious of the Divine presence there, have a heart-to-heart talk with them, and let none from your armed guard or civil officers or members of the police or the intelligence department

be by your side, so that the representatives of the poor might state their grievances fearlessly and without reserve. For I have heard the Prophet of Allah saying that no nation or society will occupy a high position in which the strong do not discharge their duty to the weak. Bear with composure any strong language which they may use, and do not get annoyed if they cannot state their case lucidly, even so, Allah will open for you His door of blessings and rewards. Whatever you can give to them, give it ungrudgingly, and whatever you cannot afford to give, make that clear to them with utmost sincerity."[31]

Multi-Directional Flow Quite often, we assume good communication as clear, concise and accurate orders and instructions from top but tend to ignore the fact that communication is good only when, along with these characteristics, it flows freely in all directions. Communication must flow not only top-down but in all directions i.e. downwards, upwards and lateral. Where downward communication conveys directives, policies, procedures, instructions etc, upward communication conveys suggestions, feedback, inputs and ideas etc from subordinates and lateral communication helps in coordination, information sharing and provision of expert views between departments.[32] In most organizations, it is not the downward communication but the upward and lateral communication which is a problem. Most organizations use rhetoric of employee involvement but keep this involvement to mere fixing of suggestion boxes at two or three places and that too as something of least priority for top management. Employees are much smarter than what management thinks about them; they observe the fate of their suggestions given through these boxes and very soon stop dropping suggestions and instead use these boxes to put everything in except suggestions. Similarly, the philosophy of obtaining input from lower cadres in the form of 'views and comments', when the decision has already been taken in the hearts of top managers, becomes a futile activity. Most of us have seen people in organizations copying 'views and comments' from other departments and pushing them upwards as they know that their effort to voice substantive suggestions will go unheard. Such organizations very soon become stagnant. Like upward communication, lateral communication is also a sore point in most organizations. Lateral communication suffers when there is lack of teamwork, cooperation and comradeship among different departments or functions. If the departmental managers talk through formal correspondence like files and memos, there are papers moving around but no communication taking place. Lateral communication comes through mutual trust and respect and understanding each other's significance in achieving the common objective. If the R&D people conceal a new product development plan from other departments in a desire to be the first in the race, this new product is likely to be bombarded by Marketing Department with customer objections, Finance may take it head on with funds scarcity, Productions may turn their back for inability to produce it with required specifications and HR may put their hands up for lack of skilled people to work on this product etc. The same very product could have become a success story and benefitted all if every department was taken onboard through excessive lateral communication.

Clarity The mission, objectives, strategy, policies and instructions must be communicated to every level in correct form and without distortion. This can only be ensured by using clear language. We see many incidents in organizations where what is intended in a message from the top level is misunderstood at the lower levels; a gap which not only invites rumors but often results in a wrong output that ruins the whole system. For example, what can be the implication of the instruction posted at a factory gate, "No one is allowed to enter the factory gate after 7:30 am."? It can either be an instruction for employees to come to work by 7:30 am or an order to the gatekeeper to stop everyone, even customers, from entering the factory after this time. Permit me to quote a joke that I read in Readers Digest and that shows how an unclear message can result in wrong output: The language teacher wrote on the blackboard, "I ain't had no fun all summer". Then she asked a youngster in the front row, "Harry, what should I do to correct that". "May be—get a boyfriend", he suggested helpfully though unclear. Another problem stems quite often from the pursuit of using flowery and difficult words in correspondence and communication in a desire to impress the recipient; a pursuit which instead of impressing the recipient, creates confusion and results in a response as understood by the recipient and not as wanted by the sender.

Response Oriented Leaders must understand that communication is incomplete unless it generates desired response from recipient. Most organizations consider mere issuance of letters, memos or messages as communication; it is not communication unless it reaches the recipients and gets a desired response. Peter Drucker says, "It is the recipient who communicates. The so-called Communicator, the person who emits communication, does not communicate."[33] A directive issued by a CEO "I expect every manager to work with full wisdom from today onwards" may not get the desired result if this 'working with full wisdom" is not understood and acknowledged by managers. Such a one-way and generic correspondence does not generate desired response and hence does not constitute communication but remains a directive. In most cases policies, directives or letters issued by superiors do not carry a feedback mechanism due to which the senders do not know whether these letters have reached the intended recipients. Such a situation not only leads to future administration and operational problems but also triggers a blame game if things go wrong. During my lectures, an HR manager of an organization narrated an incidence that one day he received a letter from his GM calling for explanation for failing to attend management meeting at the head office. The manager was taken by surprise and submitted that he didn't know there was a meeting scheduled anywhere in near future. The head office lashed back by saying that the memo was issued a week earlier and was promptly dispatched to all departments. The HR manager however did not receive this memo. The blame game continued for some time and finally stopped on issuance of warning to the HR manager for not keeping himself updated with company issues. Because of the failure to hold the meeting on time and substantial time lost during this blame game, the company got delayed in responding to an order which their competitors were battle-ready to grab. This loss could have been avoided by integrating a response measure in the memo which could have ensured that all managers had received and understood the communication. Let me quote an example of a communication with built in response measure. In Navy, operation orders are ended with an instruction, "Receipt of these orders is to be acknowledged by an unclassified signal using code word "_____". This ensures that every Commander receives the order, and is normally followed by a meeting to sort out the queries and coordinate tactical details.

Organizing

Think of a street hawker pushing his cart. It's only him and his cart, and usually no associated organization. But if this hawker makes profit and gets another cart, he cannot push two carts and needs another person to help/her. With more carts coming in, he/she will require more people especially if these carts are to sell different things to different customers in different areas. He/she will then have to talk to some wholesale shop to get things at cheaper rates, look for some carpenter shop to make a deal for maintenance of carts, search for a bigger area for parking carts at night, find a security guard to take care of carts at night and above all, find the right people with required skills to sell these things and have a plan for giving wages to these people. So is the case with organizations. Organizations need people to run the business; people working in different positions, with different responsibilities, having different skills and given different objectives. An organization, as the name suggests, is an organized system of work where people work in their designated areas with given resources to achieve designated goals. Imagine if everyone in an organization starts to work everywhere to achieve every goal then what a confusion and disorder will it be. Some important aspects requiring attention to avoid such confusion are:

Type of Organization   The debate that 'which type of organization is best' is very common in modern day organizations. The two common types that we keep hearing about are flat and hierarchical types. From these debates, one gets an impression that hierarchical type is older version and is not suitable for modern organizations and flat organization is something very good and can bring about a miraculous transformation overnight. Well, this may be true for one organization but not valid for the other just like cap of a famous brand pen may not fit pens of other brands. The debate should not be about whether the organization ought to be hierarchical or flat, the point should be that the system must be competent to achieve the objectives. Organization structure must suit the nature of organization and not just follow a management slogan. For example, many seasoned consultants criticize military's hierarchical form of organization without understanding that it cannot be flat; in Army, a Corps Commander must have Divisional Commanders, who must have Battalion Commanders, who must have Company Commanders and who must have Platoon Commanders to fight the battles in geographically dispersed sectors with diverse tasks within Corps area of responsibility. However, the organization that works best for Army may not work equally well for Navy due to the difference in the strategic and operational environment, different operating philosophy, different technology and tactics of both forces. Similarly, an organization structure that is good for a production sector company may not be a viable solution for a service sector venture, though both require some sort of organization to be there to achieve the objectives. During my stay at the Navy's HR Development Center, I met a management consultant who ran his own firm and offered a wide range of management development courses to organizations. His organization was based on a mobile phone and a laptop computer with internet connection. He maintained a virtual organization where he had contacts with organizations and trainers for finding and conducting courses. The point is that though there must be some organization to work efficiently, this organization must fit in with the objectives and working methodology.

Clarity of Structure   Whatever the type of an organization, the work must be organized in some manner; be it around functions, product or teams and there must be some rules to prevent disorder. Structural clarity means clear information about who sits where and who has what jurisdiction. No one system is best; it would vary from one organization to another. Whatever the system may be, it must deliver the desired results, must be understood by everyone and must clearly tell people where to look for answers. I was invited to talk on leadership to managers of an organization. During my interaction with a manager before the lecture, I learnt that they had two directors working at par as the joint heads of the organization, though with different areas to look after. However, since no clear demarcation of the boundaries of jurisdiction of each was delineated, they were usually at loggerheads, each wanting more power in his hands and competing for taking control of people and resources. This absence of clear order affected the entire organization which left the staff wondering as to what they should do. I focused my lecture accordingly and stressed more on the need for having a clear structure and disadvantages of lack of clarity, which quite clearly brought comforting looks on faces of many junior participants who, I assessed, were otherwise unable to raise their voices in front of top management.

Clarity of Responsibility Besides having a good organization and clear structure, there must be clear lines and limits of responsibility, clear work standards, quality and time parameters. This clarity not only ensures that the task is completed efficiently and effectively but also brings in accountability and helps in appraisal. Clear demarcation of responsibility prevents throwing the ball in each other's court. A very simple rule for having clear line of responsibility is that a person must report to one superior. On a lighter note, let me quote a friend whom I called one day on phone to ask how his new job was. In came a sudden blast from him, "Have you ever seen a wife with many husbands? If not, then come and see me. Everyone here wants me to report to him/her." A month later, he called me and said that since everyone wanted him to report to him/her, he initially tried to cope up with the demands but then decided to report to none and just do the job and give to his peon to give it to any one the peon felt like. This is what the impact of unclear responsibility is; confusion, uncertainty, chaos, bewilderedness and ultimately indifference to organizational structure.

Staffing

Organizational charts don't do the work; its people who do the work. Structures remain mesh of lines flowing here and there unless staffed with the right people. Humans are the most important resource an organization has as it is humans who manage, control and employ other resources for achievement of objectives. Points to keep in mind are:

Meeting Staffing Needs   If one person can do the job of R&D, Production, Marketing, HR, Sales and Finance in an organization then there is no need for more people to be hired and paid. However, organizations had never been and, most likely, will never be like this and will always require many people to do the job. Leaders must know the staffing needs of their organization and endeavor to provide whatever is required in whatever place. Compromises in staffing to save expenditure invariably results in more expenditure in form of poor quality, work delays, re-works, wastage, employee frustration etc. A Training Manager of an organization told me that his organization established a management development center without arranging qualified trainers and asked the manager to conduct courses using expertise of existing managers. Over the period of time, the courses became stagnant and lost their value as own people, not being professional trainers, and most of the time unavailable due to their own departmental commitments, were unable to deliver the desired results. He initiated a proposal for conducting courses on modern management skills by hiring and building a separate professional training team who would focus on analyzing training requirements, designing and developing courses and conducting courses in line with modern training techniques. After a lot of personal effort the proposal was accepted by the top management but with a remark that these courses were considered essential but must be conducted using in-house expertise as hiring of trainers would incur unwanted expenditure; a typical under-staffing philosophy which is assumed to save expenditure. These new courses were per force initiated albeit with little success and soon dropped from training program—a sheer wastage of time, energy and sincere efforts due to a wrong philosophy of cutting expenditure by under-staffing. Another form of cutting expenditure by under-staffing is to take work of ten people from five and thinking that the management is very smart. Yes, this management is smart; it very smartly affects performance standards, lowers production volumes, looses market share, leads its people to frustration and ultimately ruins the whole organization. As per my experience, organizations must question and doubt the competence of a manager who says that he/she can achieve the objective with staff lesser than logically required. This manager either doesn't know what it requires for completing the task or is thinking of over-taxing his/her people to get short-term gains or is not serious in performing the task; either case being a sure road to disaster.

Right Person for the Right Job   A donkey cart must have a donkey reigned in front with a man pulling the bridles from the cart. This arrangement can't be reversed if the cart is to work. The message here is that the aim must not be to provide merely the number of people required but provide people most suitable for the task; R&D department of a food related company must be staffed with persons with degree in food science & technology, Marketing must have people with marketing and sales knowledge, Finance cannot be handled by people other than those qualified in finance & accounting and HR cannot be practiced by people who have no knowledge of human resource management. Extra people in Finance cannot be used to fill vacancies in Marketing, Marketing cannot use spare people to work in HR and people from HR cannot be assigned to Productions to operate the machines, if they do not have required knowledge and skills. In our careers, we quite often come across situations when an unsuitable person is thrown on to us to man a position with the promise to accommodate him/her for the time being while the organization finds the right person. And, quite often, this right person never comes, forcing us to live with the unsuitable incumbent and absorb the muddle created by him/her. One may see such adhocism in organizations which make such compromises in order to cover up their HR planning follies. Poor anticipation of staffing needs, wrong staffing policies, lack of career planning and development and failure to ensure succession planning usually result in wrong persons ending up at wrong places. Such placements not only spoil the task but also break the team and lead individuals to frustration. Right person for the right job also means hiring a person appropriate for the job and not over-qualified for it. I have seen organizations inducting over-qualified persons for some job thinking that it will make the job performance better. It may work other way round as well. It is human nature to expect placement and compensation as per qualification, therefore any relegation will give rise to feelings of inequity which may lead to frustration, degeneration and may result in quitting the job. In the era of complex technology and the fast pace of changes taking place, leaders must aim for not only providing the right person for the right job but also at the right time and at the right cost. They must understand that a penny spent at the right time can save pounds later.

Training and Development Training is now being considered as an investment not an expense and good organizations are willing to invest in training their employees to transform them into a real competitive advantage. Dr. *Laurie Bassi*, CEO and a co-founder of McBassi & Company, writes that organizations which make large investments in people typically have lower employee turnover, which is associated with higher customer satisfaction, which in turn is a driver of profitability.[34] She adds that the education and training variable is the most significant predictor of an organization's success as compared to price-to-earnings ratios, price-to-book statistics and measures of risk and volatility. Organizations must invest in their people to prepare them not only for today but for tomorrow as well, not only for the job but for their personal development as well. Training must be result-based i.e. it must take into account the mission, objectives and strategy of the organization, job descriptions of the trainee, customer requirements, work tools and equipment, overall context and environment in which the trainee has to work, culture of the organization, work standards that must be achieved etc. Most trainings fail due to lack of harmony and coherence in these factors, which happens when organizations tend to import and adopt a training philosophy detached from their own needs. Leaders must also ensure that people get cross-training in different tasks so that they can understand the overall job well and also shoulder the additional responsibility in times of need. Perhaps militaries are the best example of this cross-training where an officer becomes jack of all and master of one. In navies, the system of training is such that an officer may be specialist of, for example, underwater warfare, but he is also well conversant with other domains like above water warfare, communications, navigation and can even perform the job of a security officer, mess officer, welfare officer, handling cash accounts, conducting legal inquiries, managing projects etc. Such an officer becomes an asset and can be employed on a diverse range of tasks. How about putting a Marketing person in HR department for a couple of weeks so that he/she can learn as to how the HR works in that very organization? Similar cross trainings all over the organization can help people in understanding each other's job and learn as to how each department fits into the bigger picture of the whole organization. Besides job related training, people must be given opportunities for personal development and growth in the form of general education and value-adding courses. Such development may not have direct impact on current job performance but it has tremendous effect on a person's self-worth and self-esteem and hence becomes a strong motivator. Unluckily, many organizations take training and development as a non-serious activity which is often overlooked without serious consequences. Training programs are made as a low priority, funded reluctantly, implemented unenthusiastically and followed up half-heartedly. Such trainings not only fail to bring in desired results but also result in wastage of precious resources. Leaders must ensure that there is a sound system of training and development in their organization which is given a serious focus. This system must be based on the organizations' own requirements and not on some off-the-shelf module which has been recommended by some renowned consultant.

Evaluating and Controlling

It is said that you can manage only what you can measure. For a task to be completed well, it must be measured so that it can be evaluated and controlled well. Quite often, very good ventures, strategies and processes fail to deliver the desired results due to absence of evaluation and control. Good evaluation and control allows monitoring of overall performance against the objectives which then helps in reviewing, re-assessing and re-adjusting the methods to achieve the desired end state. Without getting into literature, let us go through some common aspects which are important for evaluation and control.

System for Evaluation   Evaluation must be an on-going and a regular process and not an 'end of the year/term' thing; as is practiced in some organizations. There must be a system for immediate detection of variation or substandard performance and immediate correction to avoid wasting resources rather than waiting for specific period to end and then evaluate. This evaluation information can come from work incumbent, his/her supervisor, his/her customers and peers. The system to evaluate and assess a task to achieve the desired end can only work if the task is designed with evaluation parameters and that is only possible if objectives have been set with SMART approach discussed earlier. An objective which is vague will be very difficult to evaluate. In your career, you must have come across situations when you were yelled upon and taken to task for not doing the work as desired, though you were never told what the desired standard was. This happens when the task is given without clear standards and has no evaluation measures. You cannot measure an objective of 'improving performance' when it doesn't say where to improve, how much to improve and in what time to improve. As a simple case, to evaluate the performance of a typist, his/her job must include what to type, how much to type, with what accuracy to type and in how much time to type. Any variation in these parameters can easily be picked up. Such lucid evaluation parameters also help in selecting the right type of intervention to improve performance. For example, if a typist makes mistake in 'what to type' and 'how much to type' parameters, he/she requires more explanation and not a training course, if the problem is with 'accuracy' and 'time factor', the right intervention may be more on-job practice/training or an off-the-job refresher training course. Similarly, all jobs must be laid down in a clear manner with built-in evaluation parameters. Adopt the practice of setting intermediate milestones to see whether the task is going on time or needs some pushing up.

System for Feedback and Control   Will a thermostat be of any benefit if its input is not used to regulate the air conditioner to achieve desired room temperature? Certainly not; a thermostat is installed for the very purpose to measure the existing room temperature and then use its input to control the working of the compressor to increase or decrease the temperature. Such is the case with evaluation. Even the best evaluation system will have no meaning if it is not followed by a system of feedback to regulate work performance. This feedback in a work environment has multiple purposes; it is used for taking corrective measures to reduce variations, it is used for designing training and development programs to enhance performance, it becomes a basis for reward and recognition, it is used for career progression decisions, it can lead to decisions about changes in work system, procedures, processes and even new acquisitions. For feedback to be effective, it must be sincere, true, meaningful and timely else it will have no meaning with the people and will also have no impact on improving the system. Feedback that comprises good remarks is very easy to convey however giving feedback that conveys negative remarks is difficult as it can very easily carry negative undertones, both with the person providing feedback as well the person receiving feedback. Mind it that even feedback on good performance does not generate positive undertones if not given in a positive manner. In order to make both types of feedbacks effective, keep in mind following aspects:

Encourage frequent and open communication; giving feedback becomes easier in such an environment.

Develop an environment of trust; it helps in viewing feedback as sincere.

Hold back your prejudices while giving feedback and avoid personal attacks; it otherwise makes even the true and sincere feedback look biased.

Keep a good eye on evaluation of employees; it helps in making feedback specific.

Provide feedback on spot; it makes the feedback timely and effective.

Link the feedback with the bigger picture of the organization; it makes the feedback relevant and meaningful.

Appreciate and reward good performance in public; such a feedback reinforces good performance.

Caution and admonish for bad performance in private: such a feedback prevents hurting ego of the person and instills in him/her the urge to do better next time.

Case Study - Institute of Management Development

The Institute of Management Development (IOMD) was established in 1995 as a government institution for conducting management development courses. The founding directive envisioned it to be a leading center for management development for public and private sector managers. A Managing Director of a public sector insurance company was appointed as Director of IOMD, assisted by a team of 4 managers selected on basis of their previous managerial and administrative experience in various public sector organizations. These 4 managers were to head T&D, Marketing, HR and Finance. The institute started with around 70 employees including admin and support staff.

The first few days saw the Director and Managers sitting together trying to figure out what was to be done. As none of them had previous experience of training and development, reaching a consensus became difficult because everyone viewed the business from his own experience. Management meetings to lay down strategic objectives, to break these objectives into tasks for each department and to find ways and means to achieve these ends usually remained inconclusive. The result of this divergence was a cautious compromise and not a consensus on most of the things.

In the first few months of establishment, the IOMD hired 3 management trainers and gave them a policy guideline to design management development courses. The trainers joined heads and designed courses which, when put up for management approval, were trimmed and cut to bring them in line with management desires; the way management thought was required by the trainees. These courses were finally offered to public and corporate sector organizations through newspaper advertisements. Since public sector organizations were asked to send people for training, and the fact that there were very few institutions like IOMD, the first year responses to these courses were handsome with around an average of 150-200 trainees registering for every course. However, the course strength was never kept more than 60 due to limited training space and trainers; hence losing the remaining number of applicants. The IOMD made good profit in the beginning year and was rated as the best management development institute in the city; perhaps the only one of this stature as such institutes were not very common in those days. The success story continued for another 2-3 years which the IOMD's management attributed to their business acumen. A course certificate from IOMD was considered a master key to open all doors for employment across the corporate sector.

The late 90s saw the emergence of new entrants in the field of management development which got set with a humble start; notably less resources and support than the IOMD had. The IOMD's management disregarded chances of any worthwhile competition as they thought no one could beat their strategy and resources. Voices of concern and suggestions were raised by the trainers which, however, could not reach to the top level. The prevailing tranquility and calmness in IOMD's atmosphere received the initial jolts in the year 1998. That year brought worrying news for the IOMD when Manager T&D informed the Management Committee that the number of trainees registering for their courses had reduced to around 70-80; 60% less as compared to initial years. A cursory reconnaissance showed that people were getting attracted more towards new institutes as compared to the IOMD. The trainers pointed out the need for redesigning courses based on customer requirements, increasing the number and diversity of these courses and bringing in newer trends in delivering training. The suggestions were politely turned down by the Manager T&D with remarks that these courses had worked very well in the past. He in fact blamed Manager Marketing for not promoting these courses in a better way. Manager Marketing, on the other hand, had a prompt answer that his department was very regular with appearing in prominent newspapers. The trainers also highlighted the need for increasing the number of trainers from 3 to 5; two additional trainers with relevant industry experience to bring in diversity and new knowledge. This request, though supported by Manager HR, was turned down by the Director saying that the existing trainers can work late in the office if there was a requirement. The only happy corner was that of Manager Finance who was never short on funds as regular grant came in from government. The situation continued for another year, with every month bringing in not so good news and reducing number of people applying for courses in IOMD. The management of IOMD, however, was quite content with their management style and the immense support they had from the government. The only activity that continued with zeal and remained on an increase was the blame game for squeezing business.

As for the admin and support staff; who cared for them? They were thought to be means to achieve the ends. No one ever cared for their welfare and support, in fact, no one ever thought about them. All the trade tricks were directed at securing more benefits and perks for the management, with lower staff totally ignored. They were just required to do what they were to do including setting up the training area, keeping records, doing the clerical work, maintaining training aids, cleaning the IOMD premises, serving refreshments and tea etc. They tried to complain about their pathetic state but that was put away by the management saying that it was the habit of lower employees to seek more benefits. Later days saw an increase in electric failures during the courses, 2 out of 5 ACs went non-operational on permanent basis and other such problems appeared every now and then. Manager T&D could recall a course where the ACs did not work at all during the entire 3 days of a course and frequently tripping electric supply damaged the training hall computer.

The year 2002 brought in more bad news when 1 of the 3 IOMD's trainers left his job complaining less salary as compared to other institutes; a complaint that was termed as 'greed' by the management. The department was quick to hire replacement at the same salary; a fresh university graduate who was eager to join IOMD as trainer. In the year 2003, average course applicants came down to around 30 and Manager T&D had to use his personal links with some organizations to call more trainees at 50% subsidized rates to fill up the training hall. Manager Finance could recall two courses when half the trainees were requested on 75% discount to meet the number of required trainees to conduct the course. During one course, some of the trainees left the IOMD soon after the training and did not wait for award of certificates, saying that they had other important things to do and that these certificates did not matter much for them. While the path to decline was on,

Manager Marketing received a request from a local school for using IOMD's lecture hall for school's talent show on payment; a request that was approved after a little thought process. This then began a regular feature for the school to rent the hall every month for one function or the other. The IOMD had no objection as their own programs had squeezed with considerable gaps between two courses.

In came the year 2008. The number of IOMD courses had reduced by another 70% and 2 out of 3 trainers were de-hired. Since participation from private sector applicants had reduced to almost zero, the courses were mainly attended by public sector organizations, which were asked to keep the IOMD running. The trainees would come to attend these courses not for the sake of learning but for the reason that these courses provided them a day off from their offices. Towards the end of 2008, due to the declining performance of IOMD, government decided to convert IOMD into a Family Welfare Center that would house a child daycare center and provide training to poor women on sewing, handicraft and other jobs to enable them to earn their living. The Director and Managers were transferred back to their previous fields in different organizations. The IOMD was finally closed down and replaced by Family Welfare Center in the beginning of 2009.

For the Reader   Having gone through the emergence, performance, decline and demise of the IOMD, you must have thought about the reasons for this failure. However, keeping ourselves restricted to task skills, try to analyze the flaws and shortcomings in the light of 'Task Skills' and answer these questions:

1. Did the vision set by the founding directive provide clear destination for the IOMD?

2. Was the management able to set clear and concise objectives for the IOMD?

3. Do you feel that there was a sound strategy to move onto the road to the desired destination?

4. What was the state of communication in the IOMD? Were people able to send their suggestions upwards freely and was the management responsive to these suggestions?

5. Do you feel that the staffing state in IOMD was good or it had some shortcomings?

6. Was there a control and feedback system to provide information and awareness to the management about the state of overall business inside as well as outside the organization?

Word about Task Functions

Having gone through the task functions, you must have felt that these functions are vital for achieving the desired objectives. Strategic vision, planning, communicating, organizing, staffing and evaluating & controlling are fundamental functions which must be performed by a leader to successfully accomplish the work requirements. Absence of strategic vision leads to planning for nowhere; planning that has no sense of direction cannot be communicated effectively; lack of fundamental plan and good communication leads to flaws in organizing; poor organizing creates chaos and prevents foreseeing and fulfilling staffing requirements; the result of all these flaws makes evaluating a nightmare and absence of evaluation leads to poor control. These functions are therefore not options but compulsions to achieve the task in an effective and efficient manner in whatever field or sector the leader works.

With this, let us see some important keynotes from this chapter and then move on to the next important point of our Leadership Star i.e. maintaining the team.

Keynotes

Here are some important keynotes to remember:

- Task is the very reason for which people come and work together. It is the task which becomes the basis for compensation and benefits. Success or failure in task has direct impact on an organization's success and on its people.

- For leaders to accomplish the task, prominent functions are: Determining Vision, Planning, Communicating, Organizing, Staffing, Evaluating and Controlling etc.

- Strategic vision leads the leader and guides the organization where to invest and where not to venture. A strong and compelling vision not only sets the future destination but also energizes people to move towards this future.

- A plan provides a bridge between today and tomorrow. Unless there is a plan, an organization cannot move from where it is today to where it wants to be tomorrow. Making a plan involves setting of objectives, making a strategy and arranging resources to achieve these objectives.

- Free and effective communication is the lifeblood of an organization. Absence of communication creates vacuum which invites rumours. For communication to become a winning factor, leaders must build a supportive environment, facilitate multi-directional flow, ensure clarity and make communication response-oriented.

- An organization is an organized system of work where people work in their designated areas with given resources to achieve designated goals. Effective organizing ensures that work is done methodically, effectively and efficiently. Leaders must select the type of structure that suits the task, bring clarity in the structure and clarify the lines of responsibility.

- Staffing deals with providing the required number of people to undertake the task. Leaders must ensure that right kinds of people are available for the task. People must be trained and developed not only to perform the current assignment but also to readily undertake future assignments. Personal grooming and development must form an essential part of training and development.

- Good evaluation and control allows monitoring of overall performance against plan which then helps in reviewing, re-assessing and adjusting plan as necessary. For effective evaluation and control, organizations must have a system for evaluation and system for feedback and control.

Self-Appraisal Questions

Do you know where you want to take your organization 5 years from now? Is this desired future state known to you only or to the entire organization?

Does this desired future state compel you to work more? Are your people excited about this desired future and often talk about achieving it or are indifferent to it?

Do you have long-term and short-term objectives to achieve the desired future? Can you and your people describe these objectives in tangible terms?

Is there a clear and comprehensive roadmap which your organization wants to follow to get where you want to go to in future? Can you tell at which point on this roadmap is your organization currently located?

Can you clearly tell as to how each of your current departmental activities will contribute towards the achievement of the desired future of your organization?

Do you think your people have enough resources to achieve their objectives? What would have been 'your' performance if 'you' were to achieve 'your' objectives with the same ratio of resources as given to your people?

Do people often come to you for sharing their ideas or there are intermediary channels in between? How often your people seem well informed of each others' ideas and suggestions?

Do you often meet your people informally at their workplaces to talk to them and get suggestions? Do you meet them alone or with your staff?

Does it happen that the message which you give is understood wrong or understood partially by your people? Do your people usually turn up for clarifications in the message that you pass?

Do you ensure that your message has a built-in response mechanism which tells you how your message was received and understood by your people?

Are you and your people satisfied with the type of organization you have implemented? Is this type of organization helping or preventing you in effectively achieving your objectives?

In your organization, are there clear lines and limits of responsibility, clear work standards, quality and time parameters?

Have you provided the number of people necessary for performance of tasks in your organization? Are you aware of any short comings which you are intentionally not trying to fulfill?

Do you have some positions in your organization where the staff deployed is not fully qualified to undertake the task? If yes, then are you turning a blind eye towards this situation or trying to do something?

Do you have a formal training and development program in your organization which has your full support?

Does your training and development program flow from your own organization's philosophy, mission, objectives, strategy and work environment or it has been adopted from some other organization where it worked very well?

Do you have a system of evaluation which provides you and your people with immediate detection of performance standards or you come to know about it by the end of some fixed time i.e. one year, 6 months etc.

How true and timely is your feedback mechanism? Do your people know the basis you have assessed them on?

Chapter-4

Maintaining The Team

Importance of Team

Perhaps the most important human need after survival and security is to live among and associate with other humans. It is therefore said that solitary confinement is the most severe punishment for any human being. Maslow has put this need at level 3 of his needs hierarchy and called it 'Social Needs'. Everyone is very quick to say that humans are social animals but not so quick to understand and facilitate this phenomenon. Humans preferring to work in 'groups' is not something that has been revealed by management gurus today. It is as old a phenomenon as the mankind itself. However, the pursuit even today is to discover how this social need can be used to make humans work more effectively in groups or teams.

The enormous impact of effective teamwork is widely recognized world over. If 2 plus 2 makes 4 in logic, it is the magic of teamwork that 2 plus 2 makes more than 4, usually called as Synergy. See how individually insignificant parts join together to make a wristwatch. The combined value of a wristwatch is much more than the arithmetic sum of the price of individual parts. That's the synergetic value of a team. Look at sayings of Helen Keller and Henry Ford about team work:

"Alone we can do so little; together we can do so much." (Helen Keller)

"Coming together is a beginning, keeping together is progress and working together is success." (Henry Ford)

It is this synergy that leaders must seek for and grow in their organizations. One can find huge literature flowing from research on teamwork but the aim here is not to overload the readers but discuss some important functions that leaders must perform to maintain the cohesiveness of their team. For this purpose let us see the very basic definition of a team; it is "A group of people with interdependent skills who are committed to a common goal". Note the key words here before moving on—'interdependent skills', 'committed', 'common goal'.

Team Functions of a Leader

For the above noted elements, a leader has to ensure and build up some features into his/her team. The features or characteristics of effective teams identified by different people are diverse. Mel Hensey has identified seven characteristics of effective teams i.e. Purpose, communication, ground rules, leadership, feedback, roles and resources.[35] Kohn and O'Connell have given six traits of effective teams i.e. relationships, self awareness, empathy, norms, lateral thinking and roles.[36] Canning, Tuchinsky and Campbell of Duke Corporate Education say that managers are responsible for actively affecting three fundamental elements that are critical to team's performance i.e. aligning team's actions to specific purpose, ensuring that right resources and people are on the team and managing team's internal and external relationships.[37]

While acknowledging a wide range of attributes of effective teams concluded by learned scholars, let us pick up the few most essential features that a leader must always keep in focus (Fig-8):

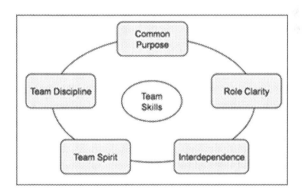

Fig-8—Team Skills

Developing a Common Purpose

This is the cardinal element of a team. Why would humans toil together or even stick together if they do not have a common purpose or goal? Hospital surgery teams have one common purpose - to operate upon the patient to get him/her rid of the ailment. Airline crew has one common purpose - to operate the flight safely to its destination while providing comfort to the passengers. A cricket team has one common purpose—to combine individual skills to win the match. A warship has one common purpose—to achieve operational readiness to beat the enemy. Imagine what would be the result if members of any of these teams do not have a common purpose—patient cut open without anesthesia and deprived of kidney instead of appendix; flight operating with passengers hungry and thirsty and landing at airport they didn't even think of; bowlers, batsmen and fielders playing their individual games as if it was not an inter-team but an intra-team match; shells, torpedoes and missiles flying all around except towards the target. Such teams not only ruin the task but also do not find any reason to stick together and soon fall apart. Such are the situations in an organization which fails in developing a common and a shared purpose. People work in whatever directions they want to work, resulting in wastage and scattering of their effort which gradually leads to weakening of the reason for working together. This lack of common direction creates dents in team unity and cohesion. Some guidelines for leaders to take people onboard are:

Explain the Bigger Picture   You must have heard about six blind men who tried to explain an elephant? It looked like a pillar to the person who touched elephant's leg, it looked like a rope to the person who touched the tail, it looked like a thick branch of a tree to the person who touched the trunk, it looked like a big hand fan to the person who touched the ear, it looked like a huge wall to the person who touched the belly and it looked like a solid pipe to the person who touched the tusk of the elephant. Though no one was right but no one was wrong as well; none had the bigger picture of the elephant. Had they known the bigger picture, they would have understood which part of the elephant they were touching and how it relates to the elephant overall. This is what happens when people do not have the bigger picture of the organization. Though they know what they do but they cannot understand where they fit into this bigger picture. Leaders must never assume that whatever seems understood to them will be equally understood by the entire team. By virtue of knowledge, experience and exposure, leaders are better poised to quickly comprehend the overall situation and understand the intricacies of the aim; a luxury not available to all the team members. Leaders must explain the organization's overall vision and the desired future, the long and short term objectives to achieve this future, broad strategy to achieve these objectives and environment in which the team is to work. Unless people know what is to be achieved, they cannot align their efforts in one common direction. Organizations with clear goals not only achieve results but also provide a strong reason to people to stick together, as said by Peter Marshal, "Give us clear goal that we may know where to stand and what to stand for—because unless we stand for something, we shall fall for everything."

Involve your People   Involve your people in the process of determining purpose or goal of the team rather than coining and imposing it upon them. The more people are involved in determining their future, the more ownership they will feel for this future and the more motivated they will be to achieve it. Purpose imposed will never be able to generate willing support. Besides being vital, involvement in determining and understanding the purpose is a thrilling experience as well and it inculcates a feeling of importance in people. It also gels people together as one team which facilitates cooperation and comradeship. At the Navy's HR Development Center, though we had objectives laid down by superior headquarters, we did an exercise to make a mission statement for us. I, as Commanding Officer, led the exercise and we involved almost everybody in the organization. A proposed statement was made and was circulated to everybody to modify it the way he/she thought it should be. The modified statements were jointly reviewed with an aim to pick up the common and agreed notions. Thereafter, these notions were integrated to make one statement. This second statement was jointly reviewed again and again to trim it to a state where there were no disagreements and further modifications. Since this mission statement was jointly prepared, everybody had a feeling of its ownership. It was proudly posted on the wall at the entrance of the building and was willingly adopted.

Clarifying the Roles

With a common purpose and clear goal in place, the next vital element of an effective team is clarity of role of every member. This is to say who is to do what and what the expectations are. In a fire-fighting team, every person has a task to do which he/she must perform so that the team as a whole can put out the fire. We all can imagine what would happen to the fire if members do not know who is to rig the hose, who is to operate the water valve, who is to enter the fire area, who is to take care of adjacent areas and who is to evacuate the wounded. The essence is that everyone in the team must know what he/she is supposed to do and there must be a caution against '*Anybody, Somebody, Everybody, and Nobody*' issue. Here are some guidelines for leaders to keep the members alive on team:

Allocate Clear Roles   Let me fully narrate the '*Anybody, Somebody, Everybody, and Nobody*' issue to explain what happened. This is a little story about four people named Everybody, Somebody, Anybody, and Nobody. There was an important job to be done and 'Everybody' was sure that 'Somebody' would do it. 'Anybody' could have done it, but 'Nobody' did it. 'Somebody' got angry about that because it was 'Everybody's' job. 'Everybody' thought that 'Anybody' could do it, but 'Nobody' realized that 'Everybody' wouldn't do it. It ended up that 'Everybody' blamed 'Somebody' when 'Nobody' did what 'Anybody' could have done. For an airline to be successful, booking office agent is to issue the ticket, boarding counter person is to issue the boarding card, flight crew is to get passengers seated and keep them safe and comfortable, navigator is to find the flight route and pilot is to fly the plane. It doesn't need a degree or diploma to understand what will happen if every task is allocated to everybody. The same example is applicable to any type of organization. Every person in an organization must be given clear roles and objectives else you will find half the people working and the remaining half loitering around and doing politics. Also, don't forget that idleness is against human nature; a person seeing no role for himself/herself soon becomes frustrated and reacts in negative ways. Therefore leaders must ensure that every member of the team is given a specific task to achieve and that the member understands the task clearly. Unclear task not only creates confusion and wastage of resources but also leads to frustration and feelings of uselessness.

Explain Work Standards   Again, coming to the example of airline, if the entire team doesn't know the work standards required then couples on honeymoon to their dream place may end up in the plane taking relief goods to a flood devastated area, flight with a capacity of 200 persons may find 250 passengers onboard quarrelling with each other for seats, plane doing thrilling maneuvers and pulling Gs like a fighter plane instead of a smooth commercial flight, passengers remaining hungry and thirsty throughout and finally getting meals 15 minutes before descend for landing. Such a chaos is certain to happen in organizations where people do not know what specifically is expected out of them, what the work standards are and what is the quality and level of output they are to achieve. Leaders must explain to their people about their duties and responsibilities along with individual work standards and resources available to accomplish the task. Individual work standards must not be vague or broad but must be specific, measurable, agreeable, realistic and time-bound (SMART). Clear work standards not only help people in putting required effort to achieve them but also help in evaluation, accountability and control. Failure in setting the exact expectations makes accountability ineffective; ineffective accountability leads to wastage of resources, low quality work and low productivity. Ineffective accountability may lead to injustice whereby the defaulter doesn't suffer and the sufferer hadn't defaulted.

All of these negative fallouts not only lead to failure in achieving task but also result in individual frustration and breaking up of team.

Developing Interdependence

The very reason for people coming together is the acceptance that they alone cannot do everything. A person cannot grow wheat, grind wheat into flour, knead flour into dough and bake the dough to get bread on his/her table every morning. One has to rely on many others for this purpose. However, the requirement is not only being aware of this interdependence but sincerely acknowledging the cooperation of others to achieve one's own aims. Leaders must create an environment in which every team member realizes that cooperation by others, at all levels, is vital to his/her own success and unless all members cooperate, no power on the earth can get the desired result. It is this cooperation which provides synergy to a team which makes 2 plus 2 not 4 but more than 4. Some guidelines are:

Explain Individual Relevance We all have been to repair shop when our watches stopped working. And we all have seen the mechanic open the case, look carefully at the machine through a magnifying eye piece and pick up one small insignificant piece which had got jammed or defective. An insignificant piece worth insignificant price but vital enough to make the expensive watch stop functioning. This is because this little piece was put there to perform some small task which contributed to the overall ticking of the watch. This is valid for any organization where every single person matters for achievement of the aim. The problem is not with mattering but it is with understanding, acknowledging and explaining that every person is relevant and does matter. A security guard at the entrance of an organization's premises will never wear a gloomy face if he/she knows how others are dependent upon his/her alertness and how it affects the overall productivity and profitability of the organization. A peon will have self-esteem no less than a manager if he/she is told as to how his/her job affects the jobs of others. If the security guard and the peon are of no relevance to productivity then why not get rid of them and save the expenditure incurred on them. And if they are relevant, then why not understand it, acknowledge it and explain it to them. So is the case with each and every person in an organization. Every person is like a piece of a jigsaw puzzle; the picture is incomplete unless every piece is put in its proper place. Leaders must understand that it is not only the line managers who deserve elegance but also the staff managers who are equally vital for organization's performance. In fact, all persons in an organization like supervisors, workers, cleaners, guards, peons etc are vital and their jobs must be acknowledged and appreciated. Explain to your people how their individual tasks fit in the big picture of the team and organization, how completion of their task affects performance of others and how their failure will trigger the failure of others. This will help them in understanding the identity, significance and meaningfulness of their individual roles. People feel motivated and become forthcoming when they know that their individual performance matters for the whole organization.

Foster Interdependence   If I remind you daily that you are very important and here is where you fit in the bigger picture of the organization, but when it comes to making you matter, I ignore you. How would you feel about yourself and the bigger picture jargon? I give you full freedom here to answer this question with the choice of your words, but in silence (see that no one is around to listen to you). Why I have highlighted this question is that this is a situation in most organizations where people are told that they are important only for the sake of saying. Successful organizations 'say' as well as 'do' to make people feel important. Sam Walton of Wal-Mart once said, "The key to success is to get out into the store and listen to what the associates have to say. It's terribly important for everyone to get involved. Our best ideas come from clerks and stock boys." Similarly, the best ideas in your organization can come from the people who are closer to the situation and not from people in head offices. Such is the state of interdependence in today's high-skill environment in which organizations are working. Finance, R&D, HR, Productions, Operations, Marketing, Logistics, Security etc are nothing without each other. If you feel that all departments in the organization are interdependent upon each other then foster this interdependence by letting every department contribute with equal magnitude. If you say that your salespersons and others are interdependent upon each other then let these salespersons contribute as well to improve the sales of the organization. And why shouldn't you make them contribute when they, and not you, have the skills required for enhancing sales? Similarly, people in each department have specific skills which can be put together to drive the organization towards its desired future.

Developing Team Spirit

While humans tend to stick together for the purpose of achieving an objective, they also have a desire for intimate relationships with those they work together. This natural inclination doesn't need to be invented as it is already there; it just needs nurturing and grooming to bloom into a flower. Team spirit, unity, comradeship, espirit de corps are some names which are commonly used for this human behavior. This spirit not only gives impetus to cooperation, performance of a common task and achievement of a common objective but also becomes a gelling force in times of greater needs and adverse situations. Militaries rely heavily on comradeship to motivate their soldiers to stay as one cohesive force when it comes to facing extremely dangerous situations and military history is full of sacrifices for comrades where soldiers laid their lives to save others. Such a spirit works like an adhesive to bind the members together in a team and move together on the road to success. Some guidelines for developing team spirit are:

Develop Understanding Remember that no two individuals are similar; each person is unique in terms of physical, emotional, mental and spiritual domains. Two persons not only have different faces, they also have different needs, different feelings, different thoughts and different patterns of beliefs. Success lies in acceptance and not rejection. And this acceptance can come only through deeper understanding of each other. Leaders must constantly endeavor to develop understanding among team members by listening to each other. Encourage people to talk about themselves, their needs, their desires, their problems, their concerns, their fears, their agonies, their thoughts and their dreams etc. Deeper understanding of each other leads to closeness which develops comradeship and team spirit. I feel that these two words have been over shadowed by today's mechanical and hi-tech environment where people come and go like robots without noticing as to who is working at the next seat and how does he/she feel about life. The so-called 'tough competition' syndrome is preventing organizations from adopting a 'peoples' shade as any time allocated for 'people only' is seen as a loss. The resultant isolation breeds loneliness among people which is the major cause of increasing stress levels and other diseases and perhaps a major reason for large employee turnovers. I am sure that if organizations calculate in longer terms, they remain more competitive, productive, viable and profitable if they allocate time for understanding and binding their people together as comrades. If you analyze, who do you want to see when you arrive in some gathering or when you come to your office every morning, and which person would you like to have at the seat next to you in your workplace? I am sure he/she is the person you understand most and he/she understands you the most. This is the gravitating power of understanding. Imagine how happy and enthusiastic your people will be to come to the workplace if they deeply understand and intimately know each other. Such is a team which has enormous synergy in it and which can do miracles.

Meet as a Team Frequently When did you go on a family picnic last time? Well, whenever you went, I am sure this picnic must have remained the point of family talk for many days afterwards and you all cherished those moments for a long time. Being together brings people together and generates good memories, the echoes of which last very long. If this is true for a family, it is equally true for a workplace. Now if I ask this question again then I am sure that you will say that people at workplace enjoyed a lot and everyone talked about it for quite some time. See, humans are humans; whether they are at home or at workplace, they have certain needs and desires, one of which is having a sense of belonging. Now it is up to the organization as to how it nurtures and satisfies this human need. In military, there are ample activities where people hang out together for few days, live together, eat together, play together and even sing and dance together. Such activities provide time to listen to each other and know each other which strengthens comradeship. I am not saying that people in organizations should sing and dance together but the message is to live as a team. Leaders must ensure that their people meet as frequently as possible; work as team, talk as a team, play as a team, rest as a team and eat as a team. Organizations must take some time out of their self-made robotic schedules and plan joint outdoor activities where people can do some physical, mental and recreational activities, and if possible, along with their families as bringing families closer makes the bond even stronger. This will provide them good common memories to cherish and make the workplace attractive to come and work. Resultantly, organizations will see lesser dead, gloomy and sad faces and more lively, happy and cheerful faces which will have long lasting effects on work, comradeship and individual motivation.

Reward as a Team   Much has been and is being written about team rewards. This reward includes both monetary as well as non-monetary rewards, which include status, participation, appreciation, recognition etc. I personally feel that rewarding the whole team for a winning performance has dramatic effects on gelling people together as a team. Though individual performance must never go unrewarded but keep in mind that in the age of interdependence, one cannot achieve success without contribution by others. A successful product that captures the market is not only because of Marketing people but it owes a lot to quality ensured by the Productions, skilled people arranged by the HR, successful design developed by the R&D, funds provided by the Finance, spare support ensured by the Logistics and ancillary support provided by many other people. Don't they all deserve appreciation and reward? Rewarding only Marketing for this product will develop cracks in the whole team which will lead to frustration and lower performance by others in future. On the other hand, team reward system that is inequitable i.e. based on cast, creed, gender and ethnicity despite same knowledge, skills and performance levels, serves as an active volcano sitting at the foundation of team work. Equitably rewarding team strengthens the sense of togetherness and emphasizes the fruit of joint effort. Leaders must ensure that the competition remains healthy and must never turn into a leg-pulling campaign, which unfortunately is the case in some organizations. Every success must be seen as 'we did it' and every failure must be taken as 'we are responsible', only then the team spirit can grow.

Maintaining Team Discipline

Last but certainly not the least is team discipline. Discipline is a very important dimension of a team as it keeps its members on track. Though the word 'discipline' has undertones of strictness but it is not always the strictness that comes in discipline; it also includes group norms that guide members to act in different situations. For example, to what extent can members deviate from standard procedures, who would finally decide in case of a conflict, how the inter-person disputes would be settled, who would have a final say on allocation of resources etc. One can see that all these situations are potentially harmful for team unity and cohesion unless they are carefully handled; therefore, this is where discipline comes in. One may think that discipline puts limits on initiative and hence it may restrict autonomy - the buzzword of modern day management. However, it is autonomy that modern day management professes not independence, and autonomy is different from independence. Where autonomy provides authority to individuals to make decisions within the ambit of overall objective, independence implies freedom to choose a different objective, which is not the essence of a common purpose. For leaders to maintain the team discipline, some aspects are:

Make Rules Visible Will it be logical if a police car stops you on a road, where there is no speed limit sign posted, and issues you a ticket for over-speeding? I am sure you will say that it is illogical since police failed in informing you about the speed limit. And, will it be logical for a manager to penalize his/her assistant for not doing the work up to the mark when he/she did not tell the assistant what this 'up to the mark' was? In broader terms, one cannot be penalized unless one knows the rules and regulations clearly. Making team rules but failing to inform others about these rules is a potential threat to team unity and cohesion. If, as a leader, you want your team to know who is to make the final decision then let it be known to all so that they work within these parameters. Rules like punctuality, preparedness, resource utilization, work standards, reporting lines, decision making, responsibility etc must be clearly known to team members so that they do not deviate from the track and sail smoothly towards accomplishment of the team objective.

Take Action against Violations   Why is it so that in developed countries, people follow the rules whereas no one cares for the rules in the under developed world? Among prominent reasons is the threat of punishment when one breaks the rules. If the speed limit signs are boldly displayed along the road but the police doesn't catch the over speeding vehicles then no one would care for these road signs. So is the case with every rule; be it theft, robbery, murder etc. And so is the case with rules in organizations; if violations of punctuality, environment, work standards etc are not penalized, these rules will lose their meaning quickly and people will do whatever they want to do. Leaders must always keep a vigilant watch for any violations and must not hesitate to take action against violators as this will show the resolve to implement team discipline. Overlooking these violations will gradually lead to weakening of the discipline, leading to an environment of disorder and chaos. The tendency on part of leaders to ignore a violation at some time and punish for the same violation at another not only loosens the discipline but also gives rise to feelings of prejudice among people; a potential bomb for ripping apart a team.

Become a Role Model Yourself   If you observe carefully, lack of discipline on the streets in under developed countries stems from disregard for the rules by the influential people and top leaders. This is a natural phenomenon; it works everywhere in a similar manner. Leaders must not forget that discipline starts from the top; you cannot ask people not to smoke in some area if you yourself smoke openly there. How can a leader ask his/her team to finish their daily tasks before going home when the leader himself/herself keeps on dragging the tasks and take days to see one file? Many rules in most organizations die their natural but quick death due to disregard by the top management. If you look around in your organization, you will be able to pinpoint rules that have lost their meaning as the top management did not follow these rules themselves. Therefore, the short message is that for leaders to implement rules, they must first become role models themselves and do not leave any lacuna that points towards their disregard for the rules.

Case Study - The Team that Got Revitalized

Mr. Khalid was employed by a large firm as Director of their Human Resource Development Center (HRDC). He had quite a good experience of working in such institutions and had good understanding of training and development. On the day he reported for the job, the firm's CEO invited him into his office and gave a warm welcome. During the meeting, the MD explained the overall vision and working of the firm, the value he attached to his firm's human resource and the importance of HRDC in his vision of making his HR a real resource for the firm's operations and profitability. Mr. Khalid felt that while discussing the existing performance of HRDC, MD's voice sounded a bit gloomy which rang bells into his ears and made him think about upcoming challenges awaiting him. He decided not to inquire more about the Center in this meeting and leave it to his own interaction and judgment when he reported there.

After the meeting he was escorted to his new office by MD's secretary. A formal introductory briefing was awaiting him which was to be attended by three Managers working under the Director i.e. Manager Training, Manager Quality Assurance (QA) and Manager Administration. The briefing comprised the firm's over all vision, HRDC's objectives, plans, schedules for meeting the requirements, major projects in hand and issues affecting performance of the HRDC. The briefing was followed by a general discussion session in which Mr. Khalid inquired about various issues. Every manager had his own answer to the HRDC's issues with apparently no consensus on cause and remedy. Though the briefing went well, however, Mr. Khalid was quick to observe uncomfortable body language and diverse frequencies of the three managers. He gave his own formal guidelines and ended the session.

The next few days provided him much deeper insights into the silent conflict between the managers. These insights came from his individual interaction with the managers, management trainers, sections' staff and other employees. His initial feelings of upcoming challenges received confirmation from this information. Further surveillance, observation, interaction and analysis revealed that the conflict had developed during the tenure of the previous Director, when the three managers were in a competition for enhancing self-importance and image-building in front of him by pulling down each other. This conflict had travelled down into the three sections and was quite obvious in day-to-day non-cooperative attitude in working of the staff.

Mr. Khalid concluded that it was not just a challenge but a huge challenge awaiting him. The initial jolt made him to think of a strategy to revitalize the HRDC; the obvious first step was to bring all the managers on one platform and make them work like a team.

After getting a clear picture of the HRDC, he met the CEO and discussed the situation with him. He was prompt enough to put up a proposal and not let the CEO get further disappointed. He, however, asked for full freedom in implementing his plan; which was quickly granted. Back into his office, he called a meeting and broke the news to managers that firm may opt for outsourcing HR development to some outside firm if the HRDC did not meet the requirements; which meant closing down of the HRDC and laying off all of its staff. He, however, told his managers that the MD had allowed him a chance to bring the Center back to profitability, failing which the organization would go ahead with this plan. The news sent quivers down the lines and everybody got his / her five senses alert to the situation.

Mr. Khalid, then, called a meeting of the three Managers along with their Assistant Managers and Management Trainers. The agenda was to find out as to how the HRDC could meet the firm's HR development plans in a better way and prevent closing down and lay off. The meeting, right from the beginning, got momentum and everybody agreed that the HRDC must stay. Mr. Khalid led the session by saying that for HRDC to stay, it must visibly perform, which required meaningful work. He then opened the debate by re-visiting HRDC's objectives. Most of the participants provided suggestions to modify or change objectives to make them deliver. Though the participants were active, however, Mr. Khalid could feel the bitterness for each other in their discussions. This, he thought, would take its own time to die down. The next few days were used for fighting out the differences on objectives. During this time, Mr. Khalid invited the participants over a dinner in a famous restaurant and announced that he would pay for it. During the dinner, he tried to involve everyone in light jokes and tale-telling. With some struggle, he managed to engage everyone. The dinner ended in good tones and everyone left with apparently good mood. The meeting next day showed some difference in participants postures; the bitterness, though still there, had become mild to the extent that they started to look at each other. He then announced that the HRDC staff would have tea breaks together daily during work hours. These breaks, he said, were just for seeing each other. First few breaks saw staff getting separated in groups according to their affiliations but slowly and gradually they started to talk to each other as they could not avoid others for no pressing reason. Mr. Khalid decided to go ahead with full force. While trying to sort out the objectives issue during day time, he announced that there would be a family picnic on next weekend on the beach for all the HRDC staff. That was something new for the people there; it certainly blew some new wind across which got spread to homes as well. The day came and the staff with families went on picnic on company arranged buses. They had a variety of activities over there in which everyone participated and enjoyed. Everyone made fun of others for doing things in a funny and weird manner. That was the first time their families met and made some good connections.

The meetings continued, however, with a significant reduction in bitter body language and grudge. The discussion went on until everyone thrashed out and agreed upon each objective. The situation after that seemed to flow as if it had found a path down the hills. Then, the time came for making plans to achieve these objectives. Everyone pooled in suggestions and ways to do things. While the plans were being sorted out and their inter-linkages were being determined, Mr. Khalid showed to Manager Training as to how he would not be able to achieve his objectives without the support of admin staff; he showed to Manager Admin that his admin would be of no use if there was no training conducted in the Center; he advised both of them that if their output was not assured for good quality by QA Section, it would never be appreciated by the firm; he informed Manager QA that his Section is running because Training and Admin are running, it will cease to function if these two stopped to work. This campaign seemed to work as they started to acknowledge this interdependence on each other and gave suggestions to each other to make things better.

With this change in situation, things moved on smoothly and plans, resources and schedules got sorted out. Mr. Khalid could then take a sigh of relief and let things be handled by his managers. The training sessions from then onwards were success stories, with training objectives being fully met because of good teamwork by all sections and trainees getting out of the HRDC ready to take on their jobs in the organization.

For the Reader   Having discussed a situation handled very well by the leader, let me ask you some questions with respect to team factors discussed in this chapter:

1. What was the situation of the HRDC team in terms of team factors when Mr. Khalid joined the organization?

2. What did Mr. Khalid want to achieve when he spread the news of closing down of the HRDC and staff lay off?

3. Why did Mr. Khalid call a meeting of the whole staff instead of the Managers heading the three sections?

4. What do you think Mr. Khalid wanted to accomplish by taking the staff out for a dinner, having combined tea breaks and the family picnic?

5. How did his efforts to build closeness affect working of the team?

Word about team Functions

Here we are; having discussed what makes teams radiate synergy. One must understand that merely coming and working together to perform some task is not teamwork and it does not acquire the magic which can make 2 plus 2 more than 4. Organizations must understand that though 'teamwork' is a good management jargon but it takes much more than a jargon to make teams deliver miracles. It requires understanding of team dynamics and sincere work to achieve the state where a group of people can become a team. And if you have noticed, making teams effective requires more of human element which necessitates investment in people and bringing them together in a natural bond which can last longer and prove successful.

Teams are made of people; if people willingly come together, they make teams very effective and if people do not come together willingly, no power on the earth can convert them into a team. With this in mind, have a quick look at the vital keynotes from this chapter and then we move on to the next important point of our Leadership Star i.e. managing the individual.

Keynotes

Here are some important keynotes to remember:

- Humans are by nature inclined to living and working in groups. Once organized into effective teams, work groups can acquire synergy which can enhance productivity tremendously. Leaders must seek for and grow this synergy in their organizations.

- Vital functions that leaders have to perform to build and maintain effective teams include a common purpose, role clarity, interdependence, team spirit and team discipline.

- A common purpose keeps a team gelled together and aligned towards a common destination. For people to come around a common purpose and own it, leaders must explain the bigger picture to their people and get the people onboard in discussing and determining the purpose.

- Role clarity implies that everyone in the team must know what he/she is supposed to do. Clearly define roles eradicate ambiguity and chaos in a team. Leaders must allocate clear roles to their people and explain the desired work standards that every person is to achieve.

- No one is independent in today's world; we all are interdependent upon each other for our personal as well as professional lives. Leaders must create an environment in which every team member realizes that cooperation by everyone is vital to success. Interdependence can be built and maintained by explaining relevance of every individual in achieving the overall aim and making every member matter.

- Team spirit gives impetus to cooperation and performance of a common task. Team spirit can be built by developing understanding among team members, meeting as a team as frequently as possible and equitably rewarding team performance.

- Team discipline ensures that members follow the common norms and rules to avoid getting de-tracked from progress. For discipline to be effective, leaders must make the team rules clear to every member and must ensure that violations are punished. However, the most important thing for leaders is to become role models themselves.

Self-Appraisal Questions

Do you occasionally explain the overall vision, objectives and strategy of the organization/team to your people? Do you involve your people in the process of determining vision and objectives?

Do you think your people know how their individual jobs fit into the bigger picture of the organization/team?

Does every person in your team know his/her exact role, objectives, work standards and resources available to accomplish the task?

Does every team member in your team know how his/her job is important for success of others and how others' jobs are important for his/her own success?

Do you solicit opinions of your team members while making decisions about parameters of their jobs?

Do you feel that your all people are one big group or think of them as distributed into smaller groups that have some differences?

Do you provide informal opportunities to your people, other than job environment, for coming close to each other?

Are your rewards individual-based or team-based? Are the rewards equitable or based on some prejudices?

Are your rules and regulations about team discipline known to everyone and implemented without any prejudice?

Do you sincerely feel that you also follow these rules and regulations?

Chapter-5

Managing The Individual

Importance of People

"Take our 20 best people and I will tell you that Microsoft would become an unimportant company" was said by Bill Gates, CEO of Microsoft. Not only Microsoft, this is applicable to any organization in the world, be it the military, public service, non-governmental organizations, corporate sector, educational, religious institutions etc. This is the place of people in any organization. It is people who willingly bring their knowledge, skills and expertise to an organization, it is people who manage and drive resources to get the final product and it is people who are the true competitive advantage of any organization. The importance of people has come a long way from being treated as an input like money and machine to a valued resource of an organization. However, the people factor has yet to travel many miles down the road to be accepted not as a resource but free and equal partners in an enterprise who deserve dignity and respect.

In this era of 'human resource', there are still incidents where this resource is treated as an ordinary input to get the output. I came across a school where academic standards were on the decline. Upon getting more information, I learnt that the teachers were changed every three years. Do you know why? Not because that the School wanted to hire good teachers but ironically due to the reason that the administration did not want teachers to become permanent employees and start getting benefits. How smart! Well, if this is the concept about people in this school, I doubt that it can ever achieve good standards. This is where most organizations go wrong. Let me ask you a question, what is an organization without people? Take people out and you will see only deserted equipment and desolate buildings, slowly becoming homes for many stray animals, birds and insects. Look what Andrew Carnegie said about people:

> "Take away my people, but leave my factories, and soon grass will grow on the factory floors. Take away my factories, but leave my people, and soon we'll have a new and better factory." (Andrew Carnegie)

Organizations that do not value their people soon become stagnant and head for degeneration. Why would people own an organization if the organization does not own them? Why would people be loyal to an organization if the organization betrays them? The simple and the only answer is that people would neither own nor be loyal to such an organization.

The importance of peoples' contribution towards organizational success needs no emphasis. Robert E. Kelley, author of "Effective Followers" says that leaders contribute only 20% towards the success of an organization; remaining 80% is done by followers.[38] John Adair sets this ratio as 50:50. Keeping in view the importance of people i.e. followers, I normally use the example of a field tractor in my lectures to highlight the relationship between leader and followers. (Fig-9)

Fig-9—Field Tractor

Front Wheels - The Leader   Front wheels exactly show how leaders contribute towards success of an organization. These wheels give the direction to the movement of tractor but they don't have enough power to plough the field. They are smaller in size but if these wheels do not turn right and left, the tractor cannot move in the desired direction and perhaps would move back and forth in just one lane. And if these wheels become deflated or stuck to one side, the movement of tractor will be haphazard, perhaps going round and round at one place. Hence, though the tractor requires mighty power from rear wheels to plough the field, correct contribution of front wheels is vital for success of the tractor.

Rear Wheels - The Followers Rear wheels tell us how followers contribute towards success of an organization. These wheels have immense power to plough the rough field but they depend upon the direction given by front wheels. Even if the front wheels are working properly, unless the rear wheels put in their power, the tractor cannot move an inch on the track.

People are the real makers or breakers of an organization. It is people who frequently come in direct contact with customers; it is in their hands to transmit whatever image of the organization they want to radiate. Management jargons like customer care, social responsibility, superb service, quality focus etc would have no meaning if people convey the message otherwise. Lofty slogans of quality and customer care by a power distribution company would go down the drain if its linemen turn up shabbily for customer complaints without adequate tools and equipment. Hence, it is the prime job of leaders to manage their people in such a way that they wholeheartedly contribute towards productivity and become the true competitive advantage. Don't forget that:

> "Highly motivated people usually reach their goals more successfully than people who may be better trained, better equipped or even smarter, but not as motivated as the former are." (World Executive's Digest)

Understanding Human Motivation

In order to manage people, one must understand people, which means understanding how people feel and what people need. This requires a complete understanding of human motivation; a subject which is not possible to be covered comprehensively in few paragraphs. However, let us go through a summary of prominent theories on human motivation to get some grip over this aspect and conclude some guidance and advice for leaders.

Needs Theory

Maslow's 'Hierarchy of Needs Theory' groups together various human needs in five hierarchical levels which are Physiological needs (hunger, thirst, shelter and rest), Safety needs (safety and security from danger), Belongingness needs (need to be part of family, group), Esteem needs (status, recognition) and Self-actualization needs (personal growth, development)[39]. From the organizational point of view, Physiological needs are met through adequate salary to buy food, a house to live, rest on job, adequate work hours etc, Safety needs are fulfilled by a secure job, safe work environment, sound health, consistent and visible policies, good order and discipline, non-coercive environment, less tension and anxiety, trust and confidence in superiors etc, Belongingness needs are satisfied through good family relations, acceptance by others, association, teams or work groups, comradeship, friendly environment, human-oriented management, accessible superiors etc, Esteem needs are fulfilled through professional competence, confidence, job mastery, achievement, recognition, reward, appreciation, power position, job titles, office décor etc and satisfaction of Self-actualization needs require encouraging creativity and innovation, participation in decision making, empowerment, delegation, personal growth and development etc. As per this theory, people move gradually up the ladder. If lower level needs are not fulfilled or disturbed, then these needs become the sole reason for effort and struggle and make other higher needs less dominant.

For the Leader For leaders, this theory provides a very good insight into various human needs, the broad categories in which they can be grouped, the order in which they appear in an ordinary person and the impact an unfulfilled lower level need has on the higher level needs. Managers must know that an employee, stuck up with food and shelter issues for his family, will find no meaning in slogans of environmental protection measures taken by the organization; a person facing job insecurity cannot be motivated by comradeship or teamwork; a person having agonizing issues in family i.e. tense relations, sick child, old-age parents etc cannot cheer up with a certificate or a 'well done'; an employee finding no self-worth or esteem in an organization will seldom get attracted by management jargons of empowerment and delegation. Leaders, therefore, must have a complete knowledge of types of needs of their employees, understand that having some needs is purely human and not greed, know as to which needs play dominant roles, learn as to why employees continuously seek fulfillment of needs, progressing from basic to higher level, and anticipate what needs may be the next to emerge among the employees. This knowledge will help leaders in understanding their employees as humans, provide them what they require, foresee what will be required and ultimately create and maintain an environment in which employees can get motivated.

Hygiene Theory

Herzberg developed his 'Hygiene Theory' and observed that all the human needs expressed by Maslow may not have motivating effect rather these needs have two distinct effects on humans; some needs prevent dissatisfaction in humans but do not lead to satisfaction (Herzberg called these needs as Hygiene Factors) and some needs have direct impact on satisfaction (Herzberg called these needs as Motivators). Hygiene Factors comprise Salary, Job Security, Company policy & administration, Supervision, Interpersonal relationships and Working conditions. These factors prevent employee dissatisfaction and bring this dissatisfaction up to zero level but people stay neutral as far as motivation is concerned. However, these needs have homeostatic effect which implies that they cease to motivate once fulfilled. And if such factors are not provided, they lead to dissatisfaction. Motivators comprise Achievement, Recognition, Work itself, Responsibility, Advancement and Growth. It is these factors which create an environment in which people feel motivated. A distinct characteristic of such factors is that, the more they are provided, the more they motivate people and the more people desire for them.

For the Leader Leaders must understand the different impacts of hygiene factors and motivators and that what needs play what roles. Organizations are most of the time focused on Hygiene Factors for building up motivation and lose the sight of real motivators. Many organizations take good care of lower level needs and expect employee motivation to shoot up. When faced with a motivation issue, they tend to provide more *Hygiene Factors* like increase in salary, more benefits, more perks, better work environment, better relationships etc thinking that this raise will improve the motivation. However, they do not know that these lower level needs only prevent dissatisfaction but do not motivate people. Besides enhancing hygiene factors, leaders must ensure that motivators like achievement, recognition, work itself, responsibility, participation, involvement, advancement and growth must also be built in the system as these are essential ingredients of the environment which facilitate employee motivation.

Achievement Theory

McClelland described three types of motivational needs of humans which are present in every one with varying degrees. These needs are Need for Achievement, Need for Power and Need for Affiliation[40]. Need for Achievement is satisfied through attainment of challenging goals and advancement in the job; Need for Power is fulfilled by authority, status and prestige and tasks which provide a high sense of power; Need for Affiliation is met through relationships, comradeship and teamwork etc.

For the Leader Humans by nature are achievement-oriented, ambitious and self-motivated. They possess the ability for creative problem solving and seek out and accept responsibility in accomplishing objectives to which they are committed. Leaders must understand that challenging but realistic and agreed objectives at all levels, starting from the top management to shop-floor employees, help people find some meaning in their jobs. These objectives, on one hand, must not be so easily achievable so as to deny a sense of accomplishment and, on the other hand, must not be so difficult that failure to achieve them sets in frustration. A more crucial aspect to this goal-setting is the true, sincere and a regular feedback to employees which can tell them about their progress. Along with the sense of achievement, the needs for power and affiliation must not be ignored as these needs play vital roles in employee motivation. These needs may be catered for by delegation of responsibility with authority. An environment of friendliness, openness, access, comradeship and teamwork can provide for the human need for association and affiliation which can enhance work smoothness and reduce tension and conflict.

Equity Theory

Adams's 'Equity Theory' is based on the premise that people compare the amount of effort they put into their work and the resultant reward they get in comparison to others.[41] Adams called these factors as *input* and *output;* Inputs comprise experience, skills, seniority, intelligence, age, effort etc and Outputs comprise pay, benefits, status, promotion, job satisfaction, recognition, job title etc. People remain motivated to perform a task as long as they see that the rewards they get in return for their effort are similar or equal to those that others get for a similar effort. If perceived inequity exists, it would create tension in an individual which in turn will motivate the individual to reduce tension. This motivation to reduce tension, according to Adams, can be manifested in six ways; altering inputs, altering outcomes, distorting inputs or outcomes, leaving the field, taking actions to change inputs or outcomes of others and changing the comparison others.[42]

For the Leader   Leaders must acknowledge that people join organizations with certain skills, information, time, expertise and knowledge which they contribute towards organizational productivity. As a natural process, people expect appropriate and equitable return for this contribution, which may be in the form of pay, benefits, status, promotion, job satisfaction, recognition, job title, advancement, self growth, opportunities for realization of potential etc. As long as they keep getting this 'appropriate and equitable' return, they remain motivated to work for such an organization. However, the moment an organization fails to create the impression of 'appropriateness and equity', people get dissatisfied. For the sake of comparison as to whether the return is 'appropriate and equitable', people compare their inputs and returns with people around them; such people being those in their own department, in other departments of same organization, same level in other organizations or even in other industry. Leaders must understand this comparative analysis by humans and try to eliminate those factors that bring in the feeling of inequity. They must make impartial policies and ensure fairness and justice in rewarding performance otherwise the sense of unfairness and inequity emerges that ruins the morale and motivation of employees.

Expectancy Theory

Vroom's 'Expectancy Theory' professes that people expect particular actions to achieve desired results and that the desired result is something worth striving for.[43]. The three variables that determine the process of motivation are Expectancy (E), Instrumentality (I) and Valence (V). Expectancy is degree of belief or conviction that a particular effort will lead to an outcome. The stronger the belief that a particular action or effort will lead to particular first-level outcome; the stronger will be the force of Expectancy. Instrumentality is the degree of belief that a particular first-level outcome will be instrumental in achieving the reward or valence. The stronger the belief that a particular first-level outcome will lead to achievement of reward or incentive, the stronger will be the force of Instrumentality. Valence is the degree to which an employee prefers a specific reward. The stronger the preference for a particular reward, the stronger will be the force of Valence. Vroom said that the overall motivation of a person to perform some task is the product of all the three variables i.e. if anyone is zero, there will be no motivation.

For the Leader Leaders must never lose sight of *VIE* process in their organizations. They can enhance the *Expectancy* by providing requisite knowledge, skills, tools, technology, time, staff, resources, procedures, processes, standards, supportive environment, feed-back, feed-forward etc to employees to perform jobs effectively and achieve the desired results. Also they must ensure that the desired results or objectives are achievable too otherwise failure will frustrate employees and the value of *Expectancy* will plunge to '0'. Beyond this point of *Expectancy* where employees' efforts play major role, the further process of motivation heavily depends on organization's management philosophy and practices. Justice, fair-play, transparency and understanding of employee needs are of vital concern to enhance *Instrumentality* and *Valence*. Where justice, equity and fair-play by management have a strong bearing on *Instrumentality* of employee achievements in getting them rewards, thorough knowledge of employees and their needs can ensure matching organizational rewards with these needs and hence enhancing the force of *Valence* for employees to perform for getting those rewards.

Job Design Theory

Hackman and Oldham studied relationship between certain job characteristics and employee motivation. According to this study, certain job characteristics help in producing certain psychological states which result in personal and work outcomes.[44] They found that 'Skill Variety', 'Task Identity' and 'Task Significance' contribute towards experienced meaningfulness of the work, 'Autonomy' leads to experienced responsibility for work outcomes and 'Feedback' provides knowledge of the results of the work. These three psychological states, in turn, result in outcomes like high internal work motivation, high quality of work performance, high satisfaction with the work and low staff turnover and absenteeism. As per the study, the strength of experienced psychological states depends upon the intensity of employees' Growth Needs Strength (GNS) which implies that employees with high GNS will respond more positively to job design as compared to those with low GNS.

For the Leader   Though people join organizations to do job and get certain incentives, it is not only the incentives that motivate people rather the job itself has significant effect on motivation. Organizations that are unmindful of this phenomenon may end up complaining about substantial staff turnover despite good pay packages. Leaders must always look inwards rather than outwards for motivation of their employees. Jobs must be designed to make them more meaningful for employees. The more jobs give meaningfulness, autonomy and the knowledge about the results, the more people become involved and own their jobs. Meaningfulness comes through Skill variety, Task identity and Task significance. Skill variety can be achieved through cross training and job rotation, Task identity can be built up by combining smaller tasks into wholesome modules to be performed by an individual or making people work as teams, Task significance can be developed by conveying the importance of every task and clearly linking tasks to over all organizational performance and productivity. Leaders must empower their subordinates and let them make decisions at their own level as the true potential of the humans can optimally work when their mental faculties are liberated rather than shackling them into carts like horses. When an individual makes his/her own decisions, he/she feels total responsibility for the outcome and hence struggles more to achieve better results. About the feedback, no one would like to work without the awareness as to where one is heading to or what one has achieved so far. Feedback not only lets one know as to how much one has performed but also informs one as to how much one should work more to achieve the standards.

'People' Functions of a Leader

Let us now move on to those functions which leaders must perform to manage their people effectively. Different literature lays down different functions that must be performed by a leader, however discussing all these functions here would unnecessarily lengthen the discourse. I have selected some vital functions that have prominent impact on leading people. These functions are shown in figure below (Fig-10):

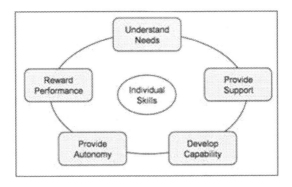

Fig-10—Individual Skills

Understand Human Needs

As said earlier, leaders must have a good understanding of human needs; one wonders as to why leaders would not understand humans when leaders themselves are humans. This is the real dilemma; leaders try to manage people without understanding people as distinct individuals which invariably results in more of disorder and chaos. What motivates one person may not motivate the other, and what motivates a person at one time may not motivate him/her at another. This is the real complexity which leaders must understand and practice. Some broad guidelines for leaders are:

Have a thorough understanding of human needs. 'What motivates humans', 'how it motivates humans' and 'to what extent it motivates humans' are the core questions which leaders must know.

Acknowledge the fact that every individual is distinct. What motivates you may not motivate others. The solution lies in empathy; seeing others through their eyes and not yours.

Understand and accept that craving for some need is not greed or lust rather a natural human need. Try to handle emerging human needs with rationality rather than snubbing behavior.

Anticipate needs of your people and try to fulfill these needs before the lack of these turn into frustration and aggression.

Provide Support

Humans are support seeking by nature; a child needs support of parents to stand up and walk, a youth needs support of friends to become emotionally comfortable, a student needs support of teachers to learn the science and art of life, a worker needs support of colleagues to learn the intricacies of work life, a person needs support of family to fulfill his/her association needs etc. The point is that humans in no stage of their lives are independent of others' support.

If that be so easy to understand, then how can we be oblivious to our people's need for our support and assistance? The problem is that what we believe, we seldom put to practice. We must understand that our people need constant assistance and support not only in their work domains but in personal lives as well. Though the underlying causes for poor performance could be many, but very prominent are the lack of required expertise and motivation to perform, as highlighted by Mager and Pipe in their performance analysis model.[45] Both the discrepancies require assistance and support from superiors and colleagues. Guidance and support to perform better along with a pat on the back can blow life into an otherwise gloomy person. A few helpful ways to provide support to people are:

> Understand that no one is absolute and every person has discrepancies along with strengths. Know your people thoroughly in terms of their strong and weak points. Make use of their strengths and assist and support them where they are weak.

> Be watchful of task situations in which your people require supervision, assistance, guidance, or coaching. Do not leave it to them to learn by trial and error as this may lead not only to wastage of resources but also frustration and demotivation of people.

Learn the underlying reasons for poor performance of your people before jumping to quick conclusions. It may not always be lack of skill but quite often lack of motivation to perform. In such situations, support and assistance can be the best solution rather than rebuke and reprimand.

Inculcate and groom an environment of supportive behavior instead of criticism and ridicule in your organizations. Commend and praise supportive behavior with appreciation and recognition.

Develop Capability

Rarely does it happen that a person enters an organization with perfect skills to readily take on the job in a completely new set of environment. This possibility is even more remote in today's organizations operating with complex technology and associated procedures and techniques. People are required to be prepared to the level where they can take on the jobs and perform up to the desired standards. This is where the role of development comes in. Development is an important aspect which leaders must always keep in mind as it prepares people both for today and tomorrow.

Organizations must not only focus on training of people to undertake their jobs but also take care of the overall development of their people in terms of their educational growth, skill enhancement, capability enlargement, personality development so that people feel elevated self-worth and high self-value. This ensures that, on one hand, the organization has a qualified workforce to undertake diverse tasks and, on the other hand, human need for development and growth is fulfilled. Militaries world-over have elaborate systems of training and development spread throughout the career of people. Courses like basic military training, basic and advanced professional courses, short developmental courses, refresher courses, staff and war courses, command courses etc prepare military people not only for discharging immediate tasks but also develop them for undertaking higher level responsibilities in future. Some broad areas where leaders can focus are:

Have a formal training and development program in your organizations. Ensure that this program has the consent and support of all the stakeholders, which includes top management, functional management, individuals etc.

Make your training realistic. Ensure that training and development flows out of your organizational objectives and is linked with individuals' job and career requirements otherwise this will never accrue the desired results.

Provide enough resources to training and development as any money spent on training is investment and not expenditure.

Ensure that training and development program is implemented and followed up in true spirit. A truncated effort not only leads to poor results and wastage of resources, it also makes people believe in inefficacy of such ventures and reduces support for it in future.

Adopt the strategy of cross training of people in different skills so that their capacity to perform enlarges. This will have two fold benefits; first, you will have people trained to undertake more than one jobs, and second, your people will develop a better understanding of the whole work which will strengthen effort alignment and cooperation.

Provide Autonomy

It is said that human mind is the most complex machine on the earth. It is this machine which invents and makes other machines work. If that be the case of human mind then what stops it from performing the best? Perhaps, it is that restriction on human mind which prevents it from working outside the traditional limits. Remove the restrictions and provide autonomy to humans to make their own decisions, and you will see an enormous explosion of the marvelous power of human mind. Jack Welch, a famous corporate leader, says, "The essence of competitiveness is liberated when we make people believe that what they think and do is important - and then get out of their way while they do it."

It was autonomy not restriction which led to stunning events like discovery of immense power hidden inside an atom, landing on moon and beyond, human organ transplant, decoding and re-engineering human genes, growing of clones, etc. Quite often good and innovative ideas are brutally murdered by unsupportive organizational environment where people are merely required to tow the preset line, perhaps becoming like donkeys pulling the cart with no say of their own; what an insulting subjugation of God Almighty's vicegerent on the earth? One is amazed to see organizations where even trivial routine changes need higher approval thereby making people totally dependent and reactive. Imagine what would happen to such organizations when the goings get tougher and they have to make quick decisions at every level to stay viable? Instant demise! Where work restrictions lead to limited output, autonomy yields enormous productivity, as said by Marshal McLuhan, "Persons grouped around a fire or candle for warmth or light are less able to pursue independent thoughts, or even tasks, than people supplied with individual electric lights. In the same way, social and educational patterns latent in automation are those of self-employment and autonomy." Though work autonomy is a complete topic to be dealt with, however, some basic guidelines for leaders are:

Decentralize decision making in your organization. Allow people to make their own decisions that affect their day to day work lives. Believe in the fact that people closest to the problem have the best solution.

Don't blindly stick to traditional ways of doing work, just because you had seen your *forefathers* doing that. Allow flexibility to people to choose work methods, procedures and schedules that suit their intimate environment. Be assured that heavens won't fall by doing that.

Listen to your people; specially listen to their thoughts and inputs that they keep suppressing inside them due to fear of ridicule and rejection. By listening to people, you can get a work solution which you were unable to discover for many years.

Groom an environment that encourages and supports innovation and out of box thinking. Reward innovative ideas that bring good results. Ensure that every idea, how so ever absurd it may be, gets to the top management once.

Reward Performance

"Money makes the mare go" and "No one is patriotic with empty stomach" are some quotes we are very familiar with. No human, or even animals, would work without reward; be it food, salary, shelter, security or other benefits etc. By the way, how many people would accept a job which provides no benefits? Would you? Perhaps not, as humans expect return for their hard work and effort and if they see that the return is either not coming or not equitable, they get frustrated and may leave the job. This reward does not mean only cash, kind and monetary benefits but it encompasses all those elements which satisfy human needs at any level. For example, as per Maslow's Hierarchy of Needs, opportunities for building association with people, self-esteem, appreciation, recognition, personal development and opportunities for realizing potential also contribute towards the total reward which people seek in their jobs.

Reward or 'compensation', as called in Human Resource Management, is a core responsibility of leaders which must never be put at the backseat. This reward must be equitable and relevant which means that one must get reward equivalent to effort, and one must get reward he/she really values. Huge research on human motivation can be a good guiding source for leaders; a glimpse of which has been covered earlier. Broad guidelines are:

Understand human needs and tailor your reward system accordingly. Provide what people need and when people need.

Focus on monetary as well as other higher level rewards which people seek in their jobs. Make jobs interesting and challenging which becomes a source for self-motivation.

Ensure that your reward system is credible, transparent and equitable and does not have any biases or discrimination.

As far as possible, ensure that your reward system does not promote individualism or negative competition rather it should promote team work.

Notwithstanding known rewards, do not forget that little kind words have immense impact on humans. Never let go any opportunity of praising your people. You won't lose anything by doing that.

Case Study—A Frustrated Team

One of my friends worked in a training team comprising 10 people from 3 different countries. This was a team which was employed by a Middle Eastern country for specialized field training of military officers; obviously the team members were highly qualified and had lot of experience in their fields. The Training Department was headed by a local officer who had three Sections under him dealing with different kinds of trainings, each headed by a Section in-Charge. This new team, though having entirely a new area of training to look after, was put under charge of one of the existing Section in-Charge, who too was a foreigner, and had some experience of this field but not as good as that of team members. Because of relevant qualifications and good experience, the new team members came with high expectations of utilizing their experience in delivering quality training to young officers. They started off very enthusiastically and provided their input and suggestions during all meetings convened by this Section in-Charge. Most of the procedures, check-off lists, handouts and course documents were prepared by this new team and given to the Section in-Charge, who got them approved by the Department in-Charge. This was the normal way of working; the team used to work and handover the result to the Section in-Charge who used to take it to Department in-Charge. There was zero interaction between the team and the Department in-Charge, and everything was done through Section in-Charge. After finishing documentation, practical training of officers commenced. The team generally worked smoothly despite facing minor intra-team conflicts, which were quite normal to occur due to different cultures and mindsets of members, but which were handled amicably by the team itself.

With the hard work and efforts of the team members, this specialized training managed to gain attention and appreciation of the top management; the smooth headway also tamed down the critics of this venture. However, this success brought in laurels for the Section in-Charge only, increasing his importance in the organization, while the team members continued to be treated like workhorses. Perhaps this growing stature made the Section in-Charge feel superior as he started to increase his control over the team and became more assertive and dictating.

With passage of time, team members noted that most of their suggestions about training objectives, methodology and schedule were either ignored or rejected by the Section in-Charge who would mostly direct and micromanage things, requiring members to follow what he said. The irony of the situation was that the Section in-Charge used to take decisions in matters in which team members were more qualified and experienced than him to find the correct way of doing things. Slowly, this observation became a whisper and then a grumble among team members who started to share their concerns with each other. On two or three occasions, they complained to the Section in-Charge about his way of working but he brushed it away by saying that he had been made in-charge of them by the Department in-Charge and he knew better what to do.

A time came when members started to openly confront the Section in-Charge for lack of freedom and participation in making decisions concerning their training area but this confrontation was constantly ignored by him. This situation adversely affected performance of the team members who reduced their efforts to mere routine level and stopped interacting nicely with the Section in-Charge. The situation went on till the time came when initial contracts of the team members expired and they were asked by the organization to renew their contracts. Out of 10, 6 members refused to stay back and left the organization despite highly attractive salary packages and perks & benefits. The Section in-Charge was left bewildered with only 4 members left and not knowing what to do to keep the venture running and keep his good reputation up which he earned for the good work done by the training team.

For the Reader   Now, let me ask you some questions in the light of 'People' functions of the leader discussed in this chapter.

1. Was the Section in-Charge able to understand the needs of the team?

2. Was the behavior of Section-in-Charge supportive for working of the team?

3. What, in your view, were the other major reasons for team's frustration? What about autonomy and rewards?

4. Could the very attractive salary package prevent most of the members from quitting the job? If not, why?

Word about Functions

Here we are; through with discussing the primary functions of a leader and getting familiar with those activities which a leader must perform in order to achieve the task, maintain the team and manage individuals. Leaders who fail in any of these functions subsequently fail in all, as these areas are interactive and affect each other. By studying the cases of unsuccessful or hated leaders, one can easily discover that the failure or the hatred was the result of failure in any of these functions where the leader unduly tilted towards one area and ignored the other. With this conclusion, refer back to the attributes of bad leaders that have been highlighted by participants of my lectures and workshops; I am sure that you will be able to link some attributes with leaders' failure in one of these three areas. As we move on with other aspects of good leadership, you will be able to establish a cause for every attribute listed therein. This awareness will help and guide you in knowing what makes people love or hate a leader and what you must do to become a successful and loved leader.

Let us have a look at important keynotes of this chapter and then move on to next vital point of the Leadership Star i.e. Leadership style, which determines how a leader performs these functions.

Keynotes

Here are some important keynotes to remember:

- People are the most important assets of any organization. Their knowledge, skills and abilities help an organization to realize its desired future. People must be treated as free and equal partners in an enterprise who deserve dignity and respect.

- In order to lead or manage people effectively, leaders must understand human needs, provide support to their people, train and develop people, provide them autonomy to make their own decisions at their levels and reward performance.

- A good understanding of human needs comes by understanding prominent theories on motivation. These theories explain as to what motivates humans and how it motivates humans.

- Leaders must provide constant support and assistance to help their people in overcoming their discrepancies and problems. To provide support, leaders must build an overall supportive environment, know their people well and continuously look for situations for providing support.

- Leaders must ensure that effective training and development programs are in place to prepare people to take on the jobs effectively and also undertake overall development of the people in terms of educational growth, skill enhancement, capability enlargement, personality development etc.

- Allow autonomy to people to make their own decisions and contribute meaningfully towards the overall effectiveness of the organization. Leaders must decentralize decision making, allow flexibility, listen to what people say and build an environment in which people feel free to give input.

- Organizational rewards must be adequate and equitable. Leaders must ensure that no effort of people goes unrewarded, reward system is tailored to suit human needs and the system promotes equity and transparency to prevent discrimination and frustration.

Self-Appraisal Questions

What will happen if from tomorrow your people stop coming to your organization/team or stop delivering required performance standards?

Do you utilize your peoples' strong points to organization's advantage and provide development to improve their weak points?

Do you have comprehensive information about your peoples' knowledge, skills and expertise? Is there a system to capture this information, analyze it, develop it and utilize it?

Does your training and development program include opportunities for personal development of your people, other than training courses required to perform their jobs?

Do you let your people do their jobs and achieve the objectives once told or you prefer to be constantly involved, like to give day to day instructions and require update and briefing from them?

Do your people regularly perform routine tasks at a set standard without much of difference and usually stay away from doing things in new ways?

Do you allow people to make decisions at their own level for small issues or you like them to ask your permission for these things?

When did you last sit with your people to listen to their ideas and inputs about work performance in your organization?

Do you allow and encourage your people to share their thoughts and inputs directly with you or you like these inputs to be sent to you through a formal chain of command?

Do you give any rewards other than salary package to appreciate people who show good performance? Are these rewards given on regular basis or are given arbitrarily?

Is your salary/compensation system equitable? Do your people get the return for what they perform or the system is based on some obvious differences? If inequitable, then how does this inequity affect motivation and performance of your people?

Chapter-6

Leadership Style

We all know what 'style' means, right? Style in simple words means way of doing something or having a distinctive form. In popular terms, it is how you interact socially, how you perceive others, how you behave in different circumstances, how you look like, how you dress up etc. In very brief terms, style is how you carry yourself in your life. This way of doing things, when associated with a leader, is called leadership style and implies as to how a leader carries out the leadership functions, how a leader deals with people and how a leader is viewed by his/her people.

Functions-Style Relationship

A simple analogy can explain this relationship. Where leadership functions are analogous to functions of human body like breathing, digestion, excretion and blood circulation etc, leadership style is analogous to clothes that we put on. Humans across the globe have same body functions and would not survive if even one function fails, however, clothes can be different depending upon environment; Eskimos require different clothes from Africans to survive in snow, Pakistanis require different clothes from Europeans to live in own climate and even in Pakistan, one requires different clothes to suit the changing weather. By this analogy, leadership functions are essential activities that leaders perform, which are fairly permanent, leadership style is the visible way in which leaders perform these activities, which should change with the environment. For example, planning is one of the essential functions; leadership style is determined from the way a leader performs this function i.e. does he/she involve people in planning or makes plans in isolation, does he/she allow others to participate in decision making or imposes decisions upon them, does he/she listens to others when setting objectives or throws the objectives on them.

Leadership Style—An Explanation

Before we move on, let me explain 'leadership style' thing a bit more by discussing something that we frequently experience.

For those who are parents, try to recall how you deal with your children of different ages? Perhaps you will be able to list down quite a few different styles. I am sure, the way you treat an infant would be quite different from how you deal with a 6 year old, and that, in turn, would be very different from how you deal with a teenager, which would be slightly different from your behavior with a fully grown up son or daughter in mid-twenties. For example, you would closely nurture and guard an infant, you would allow a little freedom to a 6 year old child but under strict supervision, you would generally give full freedom to a teenager but keep an advisory check and you would grant full freedom to your son/daughter in mid-twenties and give advice only when asked. That sounds logical and would work very well, right? I am sure you all know what would happen if you treat an infant like a teenager or a mid-twenties son like a 6-yearer—both will perish, the infant will starve due to hunger and the grown up will become a psycho case.

Now, let's take the case of a classroom. How would the teacher deal with different students? Perhaps, he/she would explain the lesson only once to an intelligent child but would take a little more time with patience to explain it to the one who is slow in understanding, the teacher would normally be kind and gracious but become harsh and strict when students misbehave, the teacher would be appreciative of those who follow school routine but would be admonishing to those who don't. Again, imagine what will happen to the class if teacher explains the lesson only once, always remains strict and harsh and keeps admonishing students just for nothing. Neither the learning will take place nor will teacher-student relationship develop and the class would become an unattractive, unimportant place for students resulting in more failures and drop-outs.

In the above examples, parents and the teacher adopted different styles at different stages and in different situations to fulfill their primary roles and functions. In case of parents, though the basic function throughout was the development of children into educated and socially responsible citizens, parents adopted different approach to handle children of different age group. And in the example of teacher, though the primary functions throughout were education and development of students, teacher adopted different approach at different times. This implies that while functions indicate your core activities, which are fairly constant, style shows how you perform these activities, which changes with the situation. In other terms, functions are 'what you do' and style tells 'how you do it'.

Well, you may ask what's so 'new' about it as this is quite natural to adopt different style in different situations and you already knew about it. Wonderful! That's the response I needed from you and that's what I wanted to bring home. Like parents and teachers, who are leaders, every leader who heads any group or organization, is required to adopt a different way of dealing with people in different situations in performance of his/her functions. Therefore, this leadership 'style' is not some new discovery or complex phenomenon but it is a logical way of dealing with different people in different situations. The way leaders deal with their people must change with situation, in fact it must be adapted to suit the environment in which a group is operating otherwise the mismatch can cause severe problems. That sounds very logical and rational, isn't it? However, logic aside, when it comes to leadership style, understanding is one thing, doing it is another, and this knowing-doing gap is in abundance around us where we see some leaders sticking to one style which they think works best in every situation.

The Theoretical Perspective

Having tried to explain leadership style through some very simple examples, let's now move on and see what formal research has to say on this aspect. In our search for various leadership styles, we come across terms like autocratic, democratic, participative, free reign leaders etc. We then generally try to learn more about these styles and create our own perceptions about these terms, may be that 'autocratic' is something very bad and obsolete in today's modern workplace, 'democratic' is something very good and sought after and 'free reign' may be difficult to practice in a competitive environment. That's how we see these terms throughout our professional lives and that's why we keep wandering what to do when the style we think is the best does not deliver results. We, perhaps, unintentionally forget something very vital which is that no one style is the best and no one style is the worst.

US Army Handbook (1973) suggests three basic leadership styles i.e. authoritarian or autocratic, participative or democratic and delegative or free reign and lays guidelines for selecting a style. There are other valid studies on leadership style which, though alone may not give a complete answer but together they provide a comprehensive view of leadership styles. The two most prominent studies are Fiedler's Contingency Model and Blanchard & Hersey Situational Leadership Model, both using different dimensions of leadership. Let's discuss Fiedler's Contingency Model first.

Fiedler's Contingency Model

Fred Fiedler suggested that leadership style must match with the favorableness of the situation at hand which depends upon three variables:[46]

Leader-Member relationship

Degree of task structure

Leader's position power

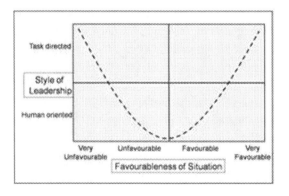

Fig-11—Fiedler's Contingency Model

Let us study Fiedler's Model (Fig-11) in easy to understand language. In this model, Leadership Style is on Y-axis with two distinct styles i.e. Task directed or Authoritarian as we go up from mid-point and Human oriented or Democratic as we come down from it. On the X axis we have Favorableness of the Situation which has four shades i.e. Very unfavorable, Unfavorable, Favorable and Very Favorable. The two axes interact to form four quadrants, with a curve running through each which indicates which style to follow in a given situation. Let us discuss each situation one by one.

Very Unfavorable Situation

This may be a situation when all the three variables are unfavorable i.e. leader's relationship with members is not good or not yet developed, the task at hand is totally new and not a routine structured task for members and leader's position power for reward and punishment is also weak. Such a state is encountered when a new team or group is formed up or a new leader is appointed to perform a totally new and non-routine task with leader having no or very insignificant reward power. Despite all odds, the leader is still required to perform his/her functions and achieve the objective. Now, how to use the Fiedler's model to determine what to do? From the position of Very unfavorable situation on X-axis, draw a straight line upwards to cut the curve and then turn left to hit the Y-axis to see which quadrant is it; in this case it will be the quadrant of Task directed approach. In such a case, Fiedler recommends Task directed or authoritarian approach which means leader should focus more on giving orders, directions and instructions and care less for seeking participation and involvement of members. This is because in such a situation the leader may not be able to get meaningful participation or involvement of members due to weak variables. Adopting human oriented or democratic approach in such a situation may not be effective and result in wastage of time and efforts. However, as the situation starts getting better, the downward sloping direction of curve recommends decreasing Task focus and allowing Human oriented dimension to come in.

This, however, is the worst quadrant for a leader and he/she must endeavor to get out of this situation as soon as possible. Though the task may remain new or unstructured for some time and leader's position power may not change, but leader-member relationship is something which a leader can and must build up quickly to move from Very unfavorable situation to Unfavorable situation which is a shade better.

Unfavorable Situation

This is a situation when at least one variable is favorable and remaining two are still unfavorable i.e. may be the leader's relationship with members is good but the group happens to be handling a totally new and unstructured task, and leader's position power for reward and punishment is also weak. Or it could be any other variable in favor like group getting familiar with task or leader getting better position power. Such a situation comes when a team or group has spent some time together, with relationship or task improvements coming in or the appointed leader getting some power of reward and punishment. The recommended style can be known by starting a line from Unfavorable position on X-axis and moving upwards to cut the curve and then turning left to see the quadrant. We come to know that Fiedler recommends Human oriented and democratic approach. This means that the leader must seek members' involvement and participation in decision making and ask for input and suggestions instead of giving directions and imposing own orders. This is because members in such a situation are inclined towards willing participation and may get frustrated and demotivated if the leader ignores their input and throws own decisions on them. As the unfavorableness of the situation reduces further, the direction of slope suggests adoption of stronger shades of Human oriented approach.

Though this is a better quadrant as compared to that of Very unfavorable situation, however, leaders must try to move on to make situation Favorable by endeavoring to get another variable positive i.e. even if the power position is weaker, group can be made to comprehend and perform the task better by better training, guidance and support. With this human oriented approach and with the group getting familiar with the task, the situation will transform from Unfavorable to Favorable, a state which is more desirable.

Favorable Situation

This is a situation when any two of three variables are favorable i.e. may be the leader's relationship with members is good and the task is also familiar and routine but leader's position power for reward and punishment is weak. Or it could be that leader's position power has improved along with leader-member relations but the task is still new and unstructured. In all cases, such a situation arises when the team has worked together for quite some time with good intra-team relations and with improved grip on task or improved state of leader's reward power. By drawing a line upwards from Favorable position on X-axis and taking it to Y-axis in the same manner as did earlier, we learn that Fiedler again recommends Human oriented and democratic approach. This implies that in such a situation the leader must try to take members onboard and seek their participation and involvement in decision making process as they are far more motivated, competent and willing to pool in their efforts and contribute towards achievement of objective. Adopting Task directed or authoritarian approach and ignoring or snubbing members in this situation is likely to turn the situation bad and result in members' frustration and disappointment. However, as the situation gets more favorable, a strange phenomenon starts to come in as the direction of curve suggests adding in a shade of Task directed and authoritarian style, which we will discuss in the next style.

Though this seems not the best quadrant but this is the situation that occurs more frequently in modern day work teams and organizations due to fast changing technology, emergence of newer work processes and stronger competition which keep the group in a state of continuous struggle. This implies that with a continuous state of complex, volatile and fast changing tasks, one of the three variables will most likely remain unfavorable. This necessitates that good leaders must always seek to maintain good work relations, involve members in decision making process, listen to them and accommodate their views and concerns, be flexible to their needs and good organizations must provide sufficient reward power to their leaders at all levels so that they can perform their functions smoothly.

Very Favorable Situation

This is a situation when all the three variables are favorable i.e. the leader's relationship with members is good, the task is also of routine type and leader's reward power is also strong. Such a situation exists when the team is fairly old and leader-member relations are good, its task is relatively consistent and of routine nature and the leader has considerable reward power. Though all seem at peak here, however, Fiedler recommends Task oriented and authoritarian approach in this situation. Strange, isn't it? But Fiedler says that if that be the situation, your members are fully ready to follow you and have a routine task to perform, they expect from you to tell them what is to be done rather than you ask them for their input and participation. In this situation, members may not find any place for input as they perform same routine task every day and also become so overwhelmed with the stature of your leadership position that they may feel hesitant to provide you input. In such a case, the leader must provide clear direction and guidance.

Though this situation looks ideal however it exists rarely in modern day organizations, where, even if the leader-member relations are excellent and the leader has strong reward power, the task at hand is fast changing, complex and volatile which makes the situation usually favorable rather than very favorable. In this environment, such a situation may exist only for a short duration but change to favorable as soon as a new challenging task comes in. I have a feeling that if such an environment exists for a longer duration in an organization, it sounds the undertones of stagnation in the work place with no challenging objectives, lagging technology, traditional work processes, routine productivity etc.

Fiedler's Styles in Practice

The model suggests four distinct situations which may lead to a conclusion that a leader lives in one of these quadrants at any given time. However, this may not be the case as, by virtue of complexity and constantly changing nature of the situation, a leader has to keep oscillating between different styles within a very short span of time. Also, a leader may adopt one style with one individual and another style with the other. For example, the leader of a team which has been working for some time on a familiar project, may have to shift focus a little more from Human oriented to Task directed approach when a new and unfamiliar project comes in but as soon as the team gets settled with the task, the leader will have to shift back to Human oriented style. Also, in a given task, a leader may adopt Human oriented or democratic style with experienced team members and Task directed or authoritarian style with new comers until they become proficient on the job.

The decision to select a style totally depends upon judgment of the leader and that is where the success lies. There is no one best style and leaders must study the environment very carefully to select a style that best suits their situation otherwise, the leadership functions, how so ever well performed, will lose their effectiveness and become unattractive and imposed mechanical drills that must be performed robotically to achieve certain ends.

Identify the Styles—An Exercise

Case-1 Mr. Raza heads a team which is responsible for looking after the financial matters of a governmental organization, a job which is very sensitive and vital for organizational work. His subordinates are professionals with varying work experiences ranging from 5 to 25 years and good training in their work careers. Their job is multifaceted which includes managing public funds of the organization, processing cases for funds for organizational activities, giving approval for financial requests of various departments, overseeing accounts audits of subordinate units and making a budgetary forecast for coming years. Though the quantum of work is immense and the sensitivities are very high, Mr. Raza is quite comfortable with his team and he gets the work accomplished with very few mistakes. He is lucky to find time to play golf in the evening as well. At work, Mr. Raza restricts himself to giving broad directions and leaves the work details to his subordinates, whom he fully trusts, but still keeps an eye on the final output of his subordinates before further necessary action. However, he is a little bit cautious while dealing with team members who have less work experience in the field or who are new entrants, and prefers to give them specific instructions with a requirement of constant feedback from them until they get a good grip over the job.

Case-2 Mr. Ahmed works in an organization and heads a team which is responsible for laying, operating, maintaining and upgrading organization's communication systems that includes landlines, fiber optics and microwaves. The organization is very large with constituent units located at dispersed places therefore this communication infrastructure is vital to organization's work. The job is very technical and requires good professional know-how to handle complex projects which can only come with required qualification, good training and job consistency. However, despite the fact that his department is very vital for the organization, Mr. Ahmed faces a severe dilemma; majority of his people come with little hands on training, stay with him for short durations and move on to other jobs. He usually has very few qualified persons who have good work experience but the quantum of work is too large to be handled by these few people. Consequently, other than those few qualified members, Mr. Ahmed usually remains very cautious with his people and prefers to give them specific directions and instructions. He normally keeps himself very close to the task area and maintains a constant watch over the performance of his people with frequent interventions when he sees them making mistakes. He says that it is too risky to leave his people unsupervised and unwatched as a lot depends upon performance of his department.

Case-3 Mr. Adnan heads a remote coastal station in a governmental organization. The place has a secondary value as most of the primary assets of the organization are located in main cities. Despite this second tier importance, his organization wants to maintain presence in the area due to some reasons but at the same time does not want to invest more than required. The task of the station is to act as a secondary station for possible organizational activities, maintain presence to show the organization in remote areas and build up good relations with locals for any future ventures. With this task in view, there are mere routine activities in the station ranging from some mails, some phone calls, occasional meetings and some visits by people of the organization from main cities etc. However, one thing which keeps haunting Mr. Adnan is that his job is insignificant and monotonous which may lead his people to frustration and stagnation. He endeavors to keep them alive by providing small incentives and benefits however he has no meaningful authority to provide such incentives and has to seek approval for even trivial amounts for his people. At work, Mr. Adnan and his team find no difficulty in handling daily work activities and usually Mr. Adnan leaves it to his people to take care of the work.

For the Reader   Having gone through these three cases, try to answer the following questions. I leave the answers to you and do not intend to provide you the staff solutions:

1. What are the respective situations existing for the leaders of these groups according to Fiedler's Model?

2. What leadership styles are adopted by these leaders in the light of Fiedler's Model?

3. What, in your view, would have happened if the leaders adopted some other leadership style?

With this deliberation on Fiedler's Model, I request you to look around or recollect your professional career in different organizations. Recall what different situations your organization went through and what leadership styles were adopted by your leaders. If you were in their place, what style would you have adopted and why?

Having seen and discussed Fiedler's Contingency Model, let's now move on and study another very important model, which is Blanchard & Hersey Situational Leadership Model.

Blanchard & Hersey Situational Leadership Model

Blanchard & Hersey Situational Leadership Model[47] is another useful model for selecting leadership style. It says that leaders should adopt their style suitable to follower development level, based on how ready and willing the follower is to perform required tasks. According to this model, there are four leadership styles (S1 to S4) that match the development levels (D1 to D4) of the followers. In simple words, this model picks up two important factors in a follower i.e. person's competence to perform and his/her motivation to perform. Though the actual form of this model is somewhat different, I have depicted it in a form that is easy to understand. (Fig-12)

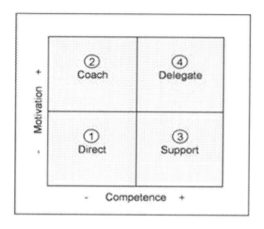

Fig-12—Blanchard & Hersey Model - Modified

Let us study the model. As said earlier, I have changed the depiction of the model to make it easy to understand. I have kept person's Competence on X-axis and his/her Motivation on Y-axis. Cross-matching of these two factors gives us four quadrants relating to four leadership styles i.e. Direct, Support, Coach and Delegate. Let us discuss these quadrants and the related styles one by one in simple language.

Quadrant-1—Low Competence-Low Motivation

This is a situation where a person's competence as well as motivation is low. This may happen when a person joins new in an organization or a group and neither has full know-how of the task nor is knit up well into the social network. Well, the two things are interlinked as well; a person who doesn't have the task competence may also get demotivated and a person who is not motivated may also not perform the task very well. However, we will restrict ourselves to the first category only. For such a person, who is neither competent nor motivated, this model suggests that leaders must adopt Directing style and focus on giving specific instructions and orders because the individual doesn't know what to do and how to do. If in such a case leaders adopt any other style, the person may become more confused, may not be able to learn or perform the task and hence get more demotivated.

Recall your career appointments or jobs when you joined new and try to figure out as to how you felt; perhaps, bewildered and alienated. What would have happened to you if in the first week your boss asked you to prepare a study report on how to improve sales of your organization? You would have felt your heart beat going out of control and your intestines wriggling. This rock and wriggle would have pushed you into deep regression and you would have felt all in the air as to what to do. On the other hand, how would you have felt if your boss called you in his/her office and explained to you the overall picture of the organization, its sales, assumed reasons for declining sales, various studies conducted on this issue, attached you with the right person for guidance and supervision and then asked you to give your own analysis after getting the required input and information? I am sure you would have felt very comfortable, highly motivated and fully energized which would have made you get settled in the organization very quickly, right? Why this difference is there in two situations? You know the reason now; you were in a situation where you joined new, you were less competent and not fully ready to perform your best. In the first case, when you required direction and guidance, your boss tried to delegate you the job, which did not go very well; in the second case, your boss preferred to give you direction and full information and attached you with an expert to provide you guidance, which worked very well.

Quadrant-2—Low Competence-Some or High Motivation

This is a situation where a person's competence is low but his/her motivation to perform is high. This may happen in two situations; first, a person has spent some time in the organization or the group and is settling down in the new environment. Though the settling down and getting familiar with the work group makes him/her comfortable but he/she still hasn't fully learnt the job skills. Second, a person although old in the organization or the work group and is motivated but has come across a new task or new equipment for which he/she has no or less competence. For both these situations, where the individual is not competent but motivated, this model suggests that leaders must adopt Coaching style and focus on briefing and showing the individual how the job is to be done and then standing by him/her like a coach to give guidance when things do not move as desired. If in such a case leaders adopt Directing style, the unnecessary close supervision may bring down the motivation level and may also affect the task performance. Also, other styles like Support and Delegation may not work as the individual lacks in task skills.

You may have come across in your career situations like this where either you had not fully learnt the new job skills or were given some task or equipment which you had not handled before in that organization. Have you been through the situation where your organization one day decided to adopt information technology for all your processes? How did you feel when you were asked to send a case form on-line for approval by your boss? Perhaps, totally blank and bewildered, as you didn't even know how to log on to company intra-net, and profoundly wanted someone to tell you how to get along with this new monster. It happened with me when I joined the Air War College as a faculty member. I was told that most of the correspondence there took place on LAN as efforts were in hand to reduce use of paper. Though I had previous experience of working as faculty member in the Naval War College and was quite familiar with computers and internet, I had no experience of working on office intra-net. For the first few days, I avoided using LAN and relied on phone for information, as I didn't know how to use LAN, and was hesitant to ask anyone as well. Although my motivation to work was high but I was new to the LAN environment. The College Commandant, very graciously, anticipated my situation and instead of taking me to task for not logging on, he asked another faculty member to go to my office and show me how to get along with this new system. This was the coaching style the Commandant used with me through another person. Had the Commandant left me at my own, the delegation style, I would have wandered and drifted here and there quite for some time and would not have been able to perform my task effectively.

Quadrant-3—High Competence-Low Motivation

This is a situation where a person's competence is high but his/her motivation to perform is low. This may happen when a person, who is quite old in the organization and knows the job well, has started to perform below standards mainly due to some pressing problem that has brought his/her work motivation down. In such a situation, this model suggests that leaders must adopt Supporting style and focus on bringing up the individual's morale by removing the cause of low motivation. If in such a case, leaders fail to identify the cause of low performance and adopt some other styles like giving orders, directions or coaching, the individual will get further demotivated and may respond in a negative manner.

Well, this is a situation which almost all of us encounter in our work careers. Various reasons, both outside and inside the organization, have impact on our work motivation. For example, a continued tense environment at home due to some domestic problem would keep a person down at work as well and affect his/her performance, also any situation or incident which a person sees as unfair like inequity, ill-treatment, prejudice, unfair return etc would bring the person's work motivation down and negatively impact his/her performance. If you happen to be in one of these situations, how would you feel if your boss admonishes you for low performance and orders you to strictly follow the check off list to ensure desired performance or puts a person over you to supervise your job and see that you don't make any mistake? Perhaps, you would feel further relegated. In such a case, your boss must try to remove the cause of low motivation, provide support to you and bring your motivation up which will automatically bring your task performance up.

Quadrant-4—High Competence-High Motivation

This is a situation where a person's competence as well as his/her motivation to perform is high. Such a person knows the task very well and can perform the task with good expertise. In this situation, this model suggests that leaders must adopt delegative style with such a person and give him/her autonomy, authority and responsibility to perform the task. If in such a case, leaders avoid delegating and adopt styles like coaching or supporting, the true benefit of the person's potential can never be accrued, which will affect his/her motivation to perform to the best. Wrong style of handling this person is likely to pull him/her down on the scale of motivation and push him/her to the quadrant of high competence-low motivation.

Recall how did you feel when you knew a task very well and were quite energized to perform it but your boss was not getting off your back and was adamant to giving you full guidance with exact steps to follow? This happens quite some times in our careers when, though we have good grip over the task and want freedom of action, but our bosses are not ready to let go our reigns and bent upon steering us like a horse. This makes us frustrated and irritated which has adverse effect on our performance.

Identify the Style—An Exercise

Affan heads a travel and tourism agency which deals in travelling, hotel reservation, car rental and guided tourism. He has around 200 people working for him in offices in three different cities. The agency's head office is in Karachi where Affan sits along with 20 staff members. His deputy is Shayan who joined the agency when it was created 15 years ago and now looks after the entire operation and makes most of the decisions. Due to his good understanding of the job and wholehearted involvement in the agency's operations, he has won confidence of Affan who relies heavily on him and allows him to run the agency. The agency's operations are networked through internet and an intra-net and most of the job is done on line with very less of paper work.

Due to rapidly expanding business, the agency regularly inducts new people and trains them on company operations before putting them on job. Shayan personally looks after all the new comers and ensures that they get good briefing of their job and understand the requirements. He prefers to give detailed instructions to them and insists that they follow the check off lists for at least one month. During this period, he regularly invites each new person for an informal talk and discusses with him/her the agency operations. The idea behind this session is twofold; first, to provide informal information about current and future operations and, second, to judge the level of job understanding of the person. He also ensures that new comers interact frequently with office staff for which he arranges combined tea breaks every week. This activity is eagerly awaited by all as it provides a good platform for a light chit chat.

Shayan thinks that one month is quite enough time to train the new comers on agency's system and operation. When he sees that new comers have learnt basics of the job and have mixed up very well with the older staff, he allows them to work independently on their work stations without using check off lists. He then keeps a distant watch on them and comes to their rescue only when he sees that things may go wrong. In such situations, he shows them how to perform the task at hand and then stands behind for a while to ensure that it is done in a correct way. He is also available to help his staff in understanding new policies and procedures. He remembers the time when his agency started the intra-net for within agency operations. Most of his people in the Head Office went blank as they didn't know how to work with the new system. He, along with the system expert, provided all the help to his people and spent hours at every work station to guide the staff in understanding the procedures.

All was going fine for Affan and Shayan till the last month when Shayan smelled something unusual. He noted that his marketing manager, Abdullah, who was otherwise a very vibrant and skilful person, had started to give alienated looks and his involvement in agency operations became limited. Shayan was quick to detect the problem and discuss it with Affan. Their minds started to get bombarded with different possible reasons for this situation; may be that Abdullah had found some better option and wanted to quit, or perhaps he wanted a raise in his salary, or he may be tired of the monotony of the job and wanted some rest etc. Exhausted with hypothesizing all the possible causes, Affan asked Shayan to visit Abdullah's house with his wife on the next weekend. Both the families went out for dinner. During the dinner, Shayan noticed that Abdullah was mostly quiet and seemed lost somewhere. Shayan tried to ask the problem but Abdullah avoided by saying that nothing was wrong. Back to his home unsuccessful, Shayan discussed the problem with his wife. She informed Shayan that Abdullah's wife was worried about their eldest son who got involved in wrong activities in high school. Shayan immediately called Affan and discussed the situation with him. Next day, Shayan called Abdullah in his office and asked him to go on a month leave and also offered his full support to sort out his problems. He did not forget to hand him over a chit with address of a famous child psychologist with an appointment time written on it for Abdullah's son.

For the Reader   Having gone through the case, try to answer the following questions in the light of Blanchard & Hersey model:

1. What leadership style Affan uses with Shayan? Why do you think Affan uses this style with him?

2. With what leadership style Shayan handles new comers? What would be the impact if Shayan does not use this style with them?

3. Why Shayan changes his way of handling new comers after one month? What may happen if he does not change his style?

4. How did Shayan respond to office staff's situation when the agency acquired intra-net? What leadership style do you think he adopted and why?

5. What leadership style do you think Shayan adopted with Abdullah? Why he chose this style?

Was the Boss Right?

In the same context, let me narrate a personal incident which may help you in understanding the impact of leadership style. I was appointed in the department of my organization which looked after the operations. As I reported for duties, my predecessor informed me that he was selected for a course abroad and was to leave soon therefore he wanted me to take over the duties as soon as possible. The urgency sounded quite logical and I responded accordingly. However, the urgency turned out to be much grave than I thought and he left the next day, leaving me totally bewildered in the office, staring at the walls like the alien who has just landed mistakenly on the earth. At 0930 hours in the morning, as I was still trying to figure out what had happened with me, I received a call from Staff Officer of the big boss who told me that boss wanted a presentation at 1300 hours on the exercise that was going on. Exercise . . . !! Which exercise? My predecessor didn't tell me anything about it. I first went totally blank but then, since I was in it, I gathered myself and asked my staff to bring me some file which was concerning some exercise going on somewhere. There was it . . . a thick antique one. As I was going through it, my immediate boss called me and asked me to show the presentation to him first at 1130 hours . . . another bomb . . . !! I hassled through the pages and started to prepare a presentation to suit the two bosses in shortest possible time. But I had my limitations - first day, new office, totally blank, no knowledge of the exercise, no knowledge of the boss and like that. I managed to prepare some slides with the help of whatever material I could gather. In came 1130 hours, though very quickly on that day, and I was at the rostrum to receive the thrashing. And I had it. It was not up to the standard as it did not meet boss's requirements; requirements which were never told to me. I made the required corrections and finally got at the rostrum again at 1300 hours in front of the big boss. Imagine what my fate was on that day; it doesn't need rocket science to conclude my situation - bombardment with full brunt and with instructions to re-present it at midnight. There I was—dejected, gloomy face, depressed, sinking heart beat, feeling lonely etc. Whatever it was, I went through it all over again, made some phone calls to participating units, saw some relevant correspondence, some signals and talked to some people. The midnight came and I managed to survive as my presentation was good enough to satisfy the two bosses. However, that day left indelible scars on my esteem which kept haunting me for quite some time.

For the Reader   Now I ask you some very basic questions in the light of the two models I have discussed above.

1.   What was my situation vis-à-vis task knowledge and orientation in the office on this very day?

2.   What leadership style my bosses used with me when they asked me to give a detailed presentation on the very first day?

3.   Was this style of leadership right? What was the impact of this style on me?

4. What do you think should have been the best style in this situation?

Word about Leadership Style

So, here we are with leadership style. You have seen how style of leadership matters and how it affects performance. If a leader has good professional knowledge but lacks understanding of leadership style, the overall impact on the organization will be counter-productive and degenerative. Research has brought out some useful styles that a leader can follow depending upon the situation; however, situation is an intangible thing and, like all intangibles, it is difficult to comprehend and interpret. A good leader is the one who continuously keeps an eye on all variables of the situation, determines the underlying factors and adapts to it quickly before it ends up into a difficult state of affairs. However, style alone does not make someone a leader; good understanding of task functions is equally vital. Imagine a doctor with good professional knowledge but poor patient handling skills or on the other hand, a doctor good at patient handling but poor in professional knowledge; both are perhaps not good doctors. So is the case with leadership.

A Big 'WHY' in Leadership

Well, let me ask you a question here. Whatever we have discussed up till now about leadership, is it so difficult to practice? Can't we just put the things right by setting objectives, planning, organizing, communicating, staffing, evaluating, monitoring, ensuring team factors, looking after our people and choosing the right leadership style etc? Is this knowledge too complex to understand or are these skills too difficult to acquire and practice? Can't we simply attend some courses on these skills and become proficient? Your answer perhaps will be 'No, not at all complex, we can acquire these skills' . . . right? If that be the case and leadership sounds easy to understand and practice then why is it so that very few leaders are loved by their people who command peoples' loyalty and faith, why very few leaders manage to influence people to willingly go till the ends of the earth, why we frequently experience short-lived leaders who get some success but do not last longer, why we eagerly keep waiting for good leaders to come and sort out our problems, why cherished and respected leaders are not found in abundance. Have you ever encountered this big WHY in your professional and personal lives? You must have wrestled with the question that what is that magic which is missing in most of our leaders due to which their leadership cannot survive beyond some time? I am sure this question must have bombarded you many times and you must have pacified yourself with some reasons, perhaps with current paradigms like complex technology, rapid change, tough competition, globalization, demanding stakeholders, boundary-less organizations, transforming work techniques, changing employee behaviors etc which have made leadership in today's organizations very difficult.

Like you, I have also been bombarded similarly many times; sometimes by this big 'Why' from my inner-self and sometimes by people who attended my lectures and workshops on leadership. These bombardments forced me to go into deep thinking, talk to people and observe good and bad leaders around us to find some homemade answer. I have concluded, as also said by Stephen Covey in his book "The Seven Habits of Highly Effective People", that to get quick results, we tend to short circuit the natural process. In order to get over-night results, we focus more on appearance rather than nurturing the deeper roots, we adopt manipulation rather than investing in ourselves and in our people, and our strategy to deal with the golden-egg goose is to slit open its stomach to get all the eggs at once rather than following the natural process. And in this crazy pursuit of unnatural process, we not only play havoc with the goose but lose the eggs as well. From my lectures and workshops on leadership, I have learnt that people are more interested in ways which grant quick success rather than learning how to dig the roots deeper. This conclusion resolved the question about the magic which most leaders lack and which makes their leadership either ineffective or short-lived. This magic perhaps lies in the charm, beauty and depth of personality of a leader, his/her those vital traits which every human loves to see for developing blind faith in their leader. By seeing and studying successful and loved leaders, one comes to know that the glittering rays which make the leadership aura beautiful are character, humility, trustworthiness, selflessness, courage, persistence, empathy etc. These traits are not some super natural powers but simple and basic human ingredients which every human can and must live with. However, since these traits and their impacts come only with time, most leaders think they don't have time for these and get down to tips, techniques and manipulation which can work faster to get results from people. They do get results but these results and the underlying relationships are short-lived as they stand on weaker pillars and not based on stronger foundations.

Your personal traits make your leadership foundation stronger and these traits are something which people want to see in you as their leader, beyond your professional knowledge and competence. Hence, now the role of leadership qualities comes in to give permanence to your leadership role. This is the next corner of my Leadership Star, but before we move on to next chapter, here are the keynotes to remember from this chapter.

Keynotes

Here are some important keynotes to remember:

- While functions indicate the core activities of a leader, which are fairly constant, style shows how the leader performs these activities, which changes with the situation.

- While there are many theories on leadership styles, the two most important are Fiedler's Contingency Model and Blanchard & Hersey Situational Leadership Model. These models use different dimensions of leadership to determine leadership styles.

- Fred Fiedler suggests that leadership style must match the favorableness of the situation at hand which depends upon three variables i.e. leader-member relationship, degree of task structure and leader's position power. This model highlights task-oriented and human-oriented styles based on favorableness of the situation.

- Blanchard & Hersey suggests that leaders should adopt their style to follower development level, based on how ready and willing the follower is to perform required tasks. The four leadership styles suggested by this model are Direct, Coach, Support and Delegate.

- These models and the emerging styles are very helpful for leaders to choose the right style in different circumstances. Style not suitable to the situation at hand leads to frustration, degeneration and failure.

Self-Appraisal Questions

Do you acknowledge that one must use different style with different people at different times or following one best style works best at all times?

Can you clearly identify the favorableness of situation in your organization in the light of Fiedler's Contingency Model? What can be the circumstances which may change this situation?

Can you tell when did the situation significantly change in the past, what were the reasons and what was your response to this change in terms of your leadership style?

When you were made in-charge of a team/committee in past, what was the situation for you, how did you handle the situation and how could your boss have made things easy for you?

When you make a team/committee for some task, how do you ensure that the situation is favorable for the team/ committee in-charge?

Can you clearly classify your people in four different categories in the light of Blanchard and Hersey's model? Do you sincerely feel that you adopt different style with people in different categories?

Is there a formal system of guidance and helping the new persons to get settled in their jobs or they are expected to take on their jobs as soon as they join the organization?

What did you do in case of your people who recently joined your organization?

What do you do when one of your competent persons suddenly starts to perform below his/her standards? Do you warn him/her to improve performance or you look in to the underlying problem and try to address it?

Do you know that if you allow competent and motivated people to work with autonomy, they can perform much better for you? If yes, then what is the state of affairs in your organization?

How many people you think are competent and motivated to work but you have not delegated them authority and autonomy to work independently? Why is it so?

Chapter-7

Leadership Qualities

Well, qualities alone cannot make you a leader but you cannot be one without qualities. As said earlier, qualities approach was the very first approach in leadership where people searched for certain traits which were present in good leaders. Later research focused more on leadership situation and group being led which added new dimensions to leadership knowledge. However, increasing focus on these two dimensions unintentionally reduced attention to qualities which relegated qualities to a lesser importance. Reducing focus on qualities, in my feeling, has inadvertently induced a notion of 'quick-fix' in leadership and given rise to a feeling that leadership can be readily learnt. However, leadership unlike driving, flying, swimming etc deals with humans and is responsible for leading people to destinations where they didn't want to go, as said by Harry Truman, "A leader is a man who has the ability to get other people to do what they don't want to do, and like it." Such a role requires deeper investment into own self before one can influence others. Believe me; humans are as smart as their leaders are. They have similar brain, eyes, ears and heart, they think in a similar way, they have similar needs, they have similar egos, they have similar desires, and why shouldn't it be when they have been created by the same Creator who created both leaders and subordinates without any prejudice. However, most leaders remain aloof of this natural conclusion and believe that they can play around with their people as they want because, in their perception, their people are not that learned and smart as they are. They tend to forget that people are very smart in discovering the hidden personalities of their leaders, knowing their true shades and disregarding what they say on the face; as said by Emerson:

"What you are, speaks so loudly into my ears that I cannot listen what you say." (Emerson)

The inner-outer divergence in leaders result in short term relationships tainted with materialism and lack of trust and faith which ultimately creates an environment of leadership crisis.

If I ask you to list down the qualities of a good leader, you will come out with a long list. Though the list of desired qualities is long but we cannot discuss all of these qualities here. However, I feel that in this long list there are some qualities without which one cannot be a good leader. I have already referred to these vital traits in the end of previous chapter. The qualities which are very essential for leaders and which I want to highlight and discuss are:

1. Character
2. Courage
3. Humility
4. Persistence

5. Empathy

Let us discuss these qualities one by one and see what these qualities mean and what impacts these have on followers.

Character

Let me begin with a famous quote of Gen H Norman Schwarzkopf about the importance of character:

"I've met a lot of leaders in the Army who were very competent. But they didn't have character. For every job they did well, they sought reward in form of promotions, awards & decorations, getting ahead at expense of somebody else...a sure road to the top. I've also met a lot of leaders who had superb character but lacked competence. They (both) weren't willing to pay the price of leadership, to go the extra mile because that's what it took to be a great leader."

Well, don't tell me that you do not know what character means and what is its importance. The reality is that we all believe in good character and know that without it we cannot become successful humans however, knowing is one thing and doing is another. For most of us, character is a good thing as long as we want to see it in others but it seems to lose its significance when it comes to us. Before going into further discussion, let us see what qualities make up our character. Without referring to any philosophical research, we all know that for good character the requisite traits are integrity, fidelity, justice, patience, simplicity, modesty etc. I am sure we do not require rocket science to list down these traits as these have been professed by every religion, desired by every civilized society, emphasized by every responsible parent and, deep in our hearts, accepted by all of us as individuals.

While we know the importance of character, we tend to circumvent it to reach our goals quickly. We think that by wearing an artificial mask of good character, we can manipulate our people and get them do what we want them to do. However, we forget that:

"Into the hands of every individual is given a marvelous power for good or evil—the silent, unconscious, unseen influence of his life. This is simply the constant radiation of what man really is, not what he pretends to be." (William George Jordan)

If, deep down into my heart, I am corrupt and dishonest to my organization but I keep giving emotional sermons to my people that honesty is the best policy, they won't listen to me as 'what I am, speaks so loudly into their ears that they cannot listen what I say.' This is because character cannot be hidden; it gets known to others without our consent. This is a reality which most of the leaders ignore; what they are from inside cannot be hidden by any cosmetic or any mask. The inner-outer divergence soon gets disclosed through unintentional and uncontrollable radiations which make people get blind to leader's slogans and sermons. Quite often, if we analyze, the failure of leadership is due to the failure of leader's character, as said by Stephen Covey:

"90% of all leadership failures are character failures." (Stephen R Covey)

As said earlier, character cannot be changed overnight; it requires time and patience to get our roots deeper into the hearts of our people. But once we succeed in getting into the hearts of our people, then no one can stop people from following us to the ends of the earth. Perhaps the best example of this time and patience is that of Chinese bamboo plant. If you sow the seeds of this plant, water it and cultivate it for whole one long year, nothing comes out of the earth. You may get disheartened but continue to water and cultivate. Yet after another year nothing comes out which may make you more dismayed. You water and cultivate for the 3rd year only to see nothing. The 4th year comes and you do the watering and cultivating with full conviction and patience. With the beginning of 5th year, the tiny plant finally emerges from the soil and shoots up to an amazing height of 90 feet in just 45 days turning into a real beautiful bamboo plant. Now, you may think, what was this plant doing for first 4 years? Lying dormant or lazy? No, not so. This plant knows that it has to grow to great heights for which it requires stronger and deeper roots to support it. For the first 4 years, it was growing its roots stronger and deeper into the earth so that when it shoots up to a mighty height, its roots are stronger enough to support it. This time and patience works with character exactly the same way. It takes very long to establish you as a person with good character but once this fact is established into the hearts of people, you then command enormous respect which helps you to lead your people where ever you want to take them.

Courage

Would you like to work with a leader who lacks courage—courage to take risks, courage to challenge status quo, courage to make bold decisions, courage to accept responsibility, courage to defend his/her people in time of need? Perhaps not, as no leader who lacks courage can ever take his/her people to the desired destination for it is courage which helps you in taking the first step. You don't lead for the past, you lead for the future and future is full of uncertainties, threats and risks. Due to the fog of future, it is rarely possible to have full and correct information to make flawless decisions. This limitation compels us to take certain risks, which requires courage and boldness. Unless you have courage to take risks, you will go nowhere and keep taking steps here and there to stay in safe zone; and leadership doesn't lie in safe zone. The turbulent and fast changing environment demands that leaders come out of safety cocoon, avoid complacency and take courageous decisions, as said:

"Courage, not complacency, is our need today; Leadership not salesmanship." (John F Kennedy)

Courageous leader inspires others and instills spark into them to face the most demanding situations whereas a coward leader turns others into cowards. Leader's courage has direct impact on his/her people; it is this courage which helps people in conceiving bold ideas, it is this courage which pushes people to break the obsolete paradigms, it is this courage which makes people bold to take the first step, it is this courage which helps people to keep fighting the odds as they move on the road to success and it is this courage which provides people with energy to stand up when they are beaten back. In fact, it is this courage which is required at every step in leadership.

"Courage is rightly esteemed the first of human qualities….because it is the quality which guarantees all others." (Winston Churchill)

An even greater courage is the courage to accept responsibility and defend subordinates when things go wrong. This courage, perhaps, is missing in most of the leaders. They are very quick to reap the benefits of success but try to hide behind their subordinates when failure strikes them. I had an opportunity to visit an organization for talking to managers on leadership. Before the interaction, I talked to one of their managers for getting an insight into the level of participants, their educational background and experience. During this informal talk, the manager informed me that their seniors are frightened to take decisions and the biggest nightmare for juniors is to take some initiative because if things go wrong, their seniors very comfortably blame them and take them to task. This environment of fear and blame had made the juniors frightened as well to take decisions, as said:

"A frightened captain makes a frightened crew." (Lister Sinclair)

I still remember my early days in the Navy when we were onboard ships for getting Bridge Watch-keeping Certificate. I was on a Destroyer commanded by a daring Commanding Officer. During high-speed multiple-ship maneuvers, an exercise which takes steam out of many experts, he used to instill confidence into us by letting us handle the ship independently. During one such high-speed and close-quarters exercise when I was to execute a maneuver, my ship was ordered to take up station from abeam to astern of a ship. I gave full rudder and speed and the ship swung violently to its new station. As my ship started to get closer to the other ship with a great thrust, my nerves began to get tense which my face failed to hide. While my heart was playing staggering beats and I was about to cow down, I felt a strong hand on my shoulder followed by a voice, "Son, don't worry and keep going. Warships behave like this and you have to have strong nerves to handle them." These words ignited a sudden spark into me which gave me immense courage to handle the war beast with full confidence, not only for that moment but forever in my career. This is the impact of courage and boldness of a leader on subordinates; it gives guts to subordinates to take risks and make bold decisions in the face of demanding situations.

Humility

Imagine a leader who is arrogant, snobbish, egoistic, who thinks very superior of him/her and who likes to stay above his/her people. Imagine another leader who is gentle, humane and compassionate and who comfortably lives among his/her people. Well, tell me what feelings you experience when you think about these two leaders. Perhaps, the first case will make your heart sink, disturb your breaths, make you scared, bring a gloomy look on your face and make your intestines wriggle. You will possibly like to avoid seeing such a leader and strangulate your great and innovative ideas. Now think of the second case; I feel, it will make your heart lighter, pacify your breaths, return your confidence, bring life back on your face and make you at peace. You will, I feel, love to meet such a leader as frequently as possible and give him/her the best of your intellect and skills.

All humans are born free and equal and all humans die free and equal. All humans have similar needs and desires; all want food when hungry, water when thirsty, shelter when exposed, safety when endangered, security when vulnerable, association when isolated and love when desolate. All crave for appreciation and recognition, all desire for respect and esteem and all aspire for performing all what they are capable of. When all humans are naturally similar, why then someone should think high of self and low of others. What can a single human do without the help of others? Nothing; without others help, we cannot even get a piece of bread on our breakfast table as it requires others to cultivate wheat, crush the grain into flour, bake the flour into bread and sell the bread in shops. If that be the case, then why a leader should assume that he/she is superior to others, above others and independent of others. If you want to test your superiority and independence, then tell your office sweeper not to come for a week and see how your life turns miserable and comes to a standstill. Or, send your peon on leave for a month and see what happens to your elegance.

If that be the case that a leader is nothing alone, then he/she must understand, acknowledge and practice this inter-dependence. This acceptance of mutual inter-dependence must then make leader gentle, humane, modest and compassionate as he/she is nothing without his/her people - people who put their hard work in making the organization flourish and leader successful. Leader's humility makes people come close to their leader, open up their hearts and minds, discuss their deeper fears and thoughts, give their best of the ideas and provide advice to leader when needed. When such a close bond occurs, the leader then gets the best from his/her people which takes the organization from goodness to greatness.

Persistence

Suppose your leader creates a compelling vision, sets challenging objectives, plans immaculately, makes courageous decisions and takes the lead but the moment goings get tough, he/she gives up and surrenders. How would you feel with such a leader? Perhaps, abandoned and betrayed—right? You will feel that even an ant, which consistently re-attempts to climb the wall despite falling down many times, is better than this leader. And, believe me, next time you will not even listen to this leader when he/she talks about some better future because, now, what he/she is, will speak so loudly into your ears that you will not listen what he/she says. On the other hand, if you follow a leader who is tenacious and consistent in his/her actions despite the complexity and difficulty of the journey, who quickly stands up after every failure and who keeps the followers going despite all odds, you will love to keep going with him/her come what may to reach your destination. This is the impact of 'persistence' of a leader; it separates a doer from a dreamer.

People constantly watch their leaders in their every action and keep making up their minds about them. Leaders who are afraid of failures breed hesitation and distrust in their people and those who face every difficulty with persistence and tenacity spread inspiration and stimulation. A quick look at all the famous leaders, in any sector, tells us that persistence was one such quality which was present in all of them. Muhammad Ali Jinnah, the Quaid-e-Azam of Pakistan, was one such tenacious leader who faced every challenging moment with immense tenacity and gigantic persistence. He commanded blind faith of his people who, despite not understanding English language, used to believe in him even when he addressed the audience in English. Look at his persistence through his famous sayings:

"Failure is a word unknown to me." (M A Jinnah)

"Think 100 times before you take a decision, but once that decision is taken, stand by it as one man." (M A Jinnah)

Empathy

I remember a medical attendant of my school days who used to give same medicine to everyone visiting the medical office. It didn't matter what the problem was, in fact he didn't listen at all and used to prescribe before even we completed our statement, "Give him two red tablets from that jar." As a result, we were reluctant to visit him and tried to fight out the illness by time and patience. The same corollary is true in a leadership system. If the leader prescribes without diagnosing the cause, it shows that he/

she either doesn't understand or doesn't want to understand the pain of his/her people.

The first step in being empathic is to understand humans. All humans are similar. Social and work status doesn't make a human different; hot weather affects a laborer as much as it affects a manager, both need safety from extremes of weather, both feel same pain when hurt, both have similar desires, both crave for comfort and happiness, both want association and belongingness and both expect respect and appreciation. This is a natural reality which most leaders ignore; some take their subordinates as means to their own ends, some look down upon them as low castes, some think they must be threatened and deprived to make them work, some manipulate them with management tips and techniques, some use them to get a job done only to abandon them later etc.

Humans, quite often, don't want sympathy; they rather crave for someone who understands their deeper problem. Once a friend sent me an e-mail, titled "someone understanding" which triggered my deeper emotional tones. I don't know the source of this mail, but here it is for you:

A store owner was tacking a sign above his door that read: "Puppies for Sale". Signs like that have a way of attracting small children and sure enough, a little boy appeared under the store owner's sign.

"How much are you going to sell the puppies for?" he asked.

The store owner replied, "Anywhere from $30 to $50."

The little boy reached in his pocket and pulled out some change. "I have $2.37," he said. "Can I please look at them?"

The store owner smiled and whistled and out of the kennel came Lady, who ran out in the aisle of his store followed by 5 teeny, tiny balls of fur. One puppy was lagging considerably behind.

Immediately the little boy singled out the lagging, limping puppy and said, "What's wrong with that little dog?"

The store owner explained that the veterinarian had examined the little puppy and had discovered it didn't have a hip socket. It would always be lame.

The little boy became excited. "That is the puppy that I want to buy."

The store owner said, "No, you don't want to buy that little dog. If you really want him, I'll just give him to you."

The little boy got quite upset. He looked straight into the store owner's eyes, pointing his finger, and said, "I don't want you to give him to me. That little dog is worth every bit as much as all the other dogs and I'll pay full price. In fact, I'll give you $2.37 now, and 50 cents a month until I have him paid for."

The store owner countered, "You really don't want to buy this little dog. He is never going to be able to run and jump and play with you like the other puppies."

To his surprise, the little boy reached down and rolled up his pant leg to reveal a badly twisted, crippled left leg supported by a big metal brace. He looked up at the store owner and softly replied, "Well, I don't run so well myself, and the little puppy will need someone who understands."

That's the empathy every human desires for. This means seeing through the eyes of others; feeling others' pain through their eyes not ours. A problem that may seem little and insignificant to a manager may have serious repercussions for a subordinate; a manager may not require a day off to take a sick child to hospital as he/she may have a second car at home which his/her spouse can drive and take the little soul to doctor, whereas a clerk may not have such options and may be the only person of the house capable of taking the sick child to doctor. If the manager doesn't understand the agony of this clerk and turns down his request, believe me that next time the clerk will hesitate to come to this manager for whatever problem he might have and will lose faith in the leader.

> "The day soldiers stop bringing you their problems is the day you have stopped leading them. They have either lost confidence that you can help them or concluded that you don't care. Either case is a failure of leadership." (Gen Colin Powell)

Leaders must understand that empathy goes beyond typical welfare. Free meal for subordinates after an exhausting task is not empathy but a basic human need; empathy means understanding the inner desires and problems of subordinates and then acting wholeheartedly to fulfill these desires and solving these problems. Quite often, 'know your men' philosophy is taken wrong both in military and corporate world. Leaders believe that 'know you men' implies knowing the name of the subordinate, his/her rank, qualifications, time in the organization, address of house, number of children etc. This is merely 'personal information' and not 'knowing the men'; 'knowing the men' means understanding each person as a unique human, knowing the needs, understanding the problems and pains, knowing the desires and dreams and then helping him/her out to fulfill these needs, solve the problems and realize the desires and dreams.

"To lead the people, walk behind them." (Lao Tzu)

Humans are hungry for kindness and respect. Little words of kindness and respect which may not take away anything from a leader may have tremendous impact on subordinates. Have you ever seen the impact of word 'thank you' on the face of a peon who serves you tea or brings you a file? Most of us just reply with cold words like 'put it there' and do not even look at these people as we are busy with some important thing; something which, we think, is more important than humans. We tend to forget that it is humans, not things, which make an organization successful, it is people who manage and control all other resources of the organization and it is people who run and maintain the systems and processes.

"Kind words can be short and easy to speak, but their echoes are truly endless." (Mother Theresa)

Dealing with your subordinates with empathy triggers an inner fire into them which transforms them from mere 'personnel' to 'human resource' and energizes them to perform miraculously. Such a human resource then becomes a sustainable competitive advantage and can make the organization invincible; be it a corporate organization or military force.

"In war, $3/4^{th}$ turns on personal character and relations; the balance of manpower and materials counts only for the remaining quarter." (Napoleon)

Leaders, who know their men and know their needs and desires, and sincerely work for the betterment of their men, are lucky to have a highly motivated workforce which can take a bold step when required, which can face any challenge that comes in their way, which can overcome any hurdle that tries to stop them from moving on, which can keep going despite suffering, which can bravely stand up even if beaten back and which can successfully reach the destination and fulfill the mission. Therefore, the advice to all leaders is:

"Take care of your people; they will take care of your mission." (Admiral Nelson)

Keynotes

Here are some important keynotes to remember:

- Good qualities alone cannot make you a leader but you cannot be one without good qualities. Qualities provide a strong foundation for leadership and gives strength to the personality of a leader.

- Though there are many leadership qualities listed by prominent researchers, but the most vital are: character, courage, humility, persistence and empathy.

- Positive traits which count prominently in making character good and strong are integrity, fidelity, justice, patience, simplicity and modesty etc. Character cannot be acquired overnight, it requires long term investment. Also, character cannot be hidden, it gets radiated to others. Without backed by a solid character, leadership either fails or tends to be short-lived.

- Courage is a very essential quality of leadership; courage to take stand when goings get tough, courage to take bold decisions, courage to avoid complacency and courage to accept responsibility. Courageous leaders breed courageous people and without courage you cannot move an inch forward to your desired destination.

- Humility means accepting one's self like any other human being and avoiding being egoistic, arrogant and snobbish. Leaders who are arrogant make people scared to come close and give ideas and advice. Leaders who show humility, make their people comfortable in coming close and sharing their hearts and minds with the leader. This bond makes people give their best of intellect and skills for the task which ultimately brings success for the organization.

- Persistence shows how committed and steadfast a leader is. Leaders, who back out when met with a failure, lack devoted and enthusiastic subordinates. Leaders who are tenacious and consistent command love and faith of their people which keeps the team moving forward, come what may, to reach the destination.

- Empathy means seeing through the eyes of others. This implies understanding humans through their eyes and not yours. Empathy has tremendous and long lasting impact on people. Humans, quite often, don't want sympathy; they rather crave for someone who understands them. Empathic leaders are loved, respected and followed wholeheartedly.

Self-Appraisal Questions

What qualities do you want to see in your leader? Do you endeavor to develop same qualities in you?

Can you tell what qualities your some previous leader lacked which made you dislike him/her? Do you try to avoid such a situation with your people?

Do you sincerely feel that you do not merely pose a good personality in front of your people? Do you fully know your shortcomings and do something to overcome these problems?

Do you readily want return from your people if you do something good for their betterment or you do it and not mention it?

Do your people hesitate to come close to you and talk openly with you? If yes, then what could be the reason?

Do your people readily stand up with you and support you for whatever you say or they are reluctant and very cautious?

Do you feel that you have guts to stand up and talk about some wrong policy, procedure and objective and give the solution for it or accept it as it is and try to obey it because you think you should go with the flow of the system?

Do you allow your people to take risky decisions or you have a doubt that they may go wrong and make situation difficult for you?

How often do you sit with your people in their own environment? Do you sincerely feel that there is a distance between you and your people? If yes, then do you know that this distance is eating up your organization and preventing it from achieving great heights?

When you do not fully achieve what you wanted, do you change your pursuit or you go again after it till you succeed?

Do you fully understand your peoples' needs, desires and problems? Do you work for their benefits as you think is good or you work to solve their problems as they want you to do?

The Last Word

Here we are at the end of our journey through leadership enigma. I hope that this journey has given you some insight into leadership; a concept that has become not only a difficult proposition but a mystery for many of us.

Though the humans are product of nature, however, the dilemma is that we believe less in nature and more into unnatural process. As said by Stephen Covey is his book, "Seven Habits of Highly Effective People", we tend to forget the law of the farm, where sowing has to come before harvesting. In a similar manner, wisdom has to be preceded by knowledge, success has to be preceded by toil, trust has to be preceded by trust worthiness, love has to be preceded by empathy, getting respect has to be preceded by giving respect and leadership has to be preceded by understanding leadership. However, in pursuit of quick gains, we tend to short circuit the nature by manipulation based on some tips and techniques. We desire to gain the height of Chinese bamboo plant without getting our roots deeper into soil. We try to lead humans while ignoring to understand humans. The natural result of this unnatural process is frustration, disappointment, dissatisfaction, discontent etc in most of today's organizations. The blame, however, is easily attributed to leadership theory and research and we quickly leap over to substitutes for leadership. My question is, are humans a disease and is leadership an antibiotic that if it doesn't work, we can switch to alternate medicines?

The problem is that we take leadership as a form of antibiotic and expect it to deliver results in two to three days, and stop taking it when it cures the problem. Like antibiotics, we believe in choosing the specific medicine with the specific dose for a specific time to get the desired results. This is where we fault, and this is not the fault of leadership but the problem with our paradigms and perceptions; paradigms of instant meals, quick services, faster gains, rapidly fattening bottom-lines, short cuts etc. These paradigms make leaders handle everything with a quick fix approach, be it tools, technology, processes, systems, products, services, buildings and even humans etc. They look for a simple check off list which they can tick and get the result, not understanding that humans, unlike things, cannot be handled through this approach. Humans are free and equal souls which must be lead with freedom, respect and equality and not with control, disrespect and deprivation strategy. Humans do not need threat, fear and deprivation but need trust and confidence to open up, to let others influence them and to make them work. And this is the approach which today's leadership needs to adopt rather than looking for a quick fix over-night formula to handle people. This trust and confidence is not achieved by cosmetics but built over a long time and once built, it stays forever and produces miracles. This long time investment requires understanding of human nature, human needs and desires and human problems and pains.

Leadership is not only some qualities that we acquire them or put them on for some time and get the desired results without any further toil. Leadership is also not only a matter of adopting some suitable style to handle humans without having any deeper roots into their hearts. Leadership is not a matter of functions alone which we perform efficiently to reach our goals without getting wholehearted acceptance by our people. Leadership, in fact, is a commitment, is a pledge, is an oath and is a promise to take the people to a better future; it does not require tips and techniques but it requires investment into own self and into people to win their trust and faith so that they willingly commence the journey onto the unknown road to their desired destination.

Let me end this book with some portions of famous epistle of Hazrat Ali (May Allah be pleased with him), as referred before and then give my own definition of leadership:[48]

"Be it known to you, O Malik, that I am sending you as Governor to a country which in the past has experienced both just and unjust rule. Men will scrutinize your actions with a searching eye, even as you used to scrutinize the actions of those before you, and speak of you, even as you did speak of them. The fact is that the public speak well of only those who do good and it is they who furnish the proof of your actions. Hence the richest treasure that you may covet should be the treasure of good deeds. Keep your desires under control and deny yourself what has been prohibited, for, by such abstinence alone, will you be able to distinguish between what is good for them and what is not."

"Develop in your heart the feeling of love for your people and let it be a source of kindliness and blessing to them. Do not behave with them like a barbarian, and do not appropriate to yourself that which belongs to them. Remember that the citizens of the state are of two categories. They are either your brethren in religion or your brethren in kind. They are subject to infirmities and liable to commit mistakes. Some indeed do commit mistakes. But forgive them even as you would like Allah to forgive you. Bear in mind that you are placed over them, even as I am placed over you. And then there is Allah even above who has given you the position of a Governor in order that you may look after those under you and be sufficient unto them. And you will be judged by what you do for them."

"Care for your people with the tenderness with which you care for your children, and do not talk before them of any good that you might have done to them, nor disregard any expression of affection which they show in return; for such conduct inspires loyalty, devotion and goodwill. Attend to every little of their wants not resting content with some general help that you may have given to them, for sometimes timely attention to a little want of theirs brings them immense relief. Surely these people will not forget you in your own hour of need."

Having gathered, arranged and presented my thoughts on leadership through this book, here is the definition, which I feel, takes into account most aspects that are vital for a successful leadership.

"Leadership is a process in which a person influences others through competence and qualities, with trust in each other, to willingly work together to achieve a common task that satisfies group and individual needs."

I sincerely wish you fair winds and following seas in your role as present and future leaders of your organizations.

Endnotes

1   Burns, J. M. (1978) *Leadership*, New York, Harper & Row, pp.2

2   Ibid

3   Luthans, F. (2005) *Organizational Behavior*, 10th edition, New York, McGraw-Hill, pp. 564-565

4   Maxwell, John C. (1999) *The 21 Indispensible Qualities of a Leader*, Tennessee (USA), Thomas Nelson, pp. IX

5   *www.scribd.com/doc/8949696/Leadership-ITL1 (accessed 21 Oct 2010)*

6   Northouse (2004) quoted in website of University of Exeter, Center for Leadership Studies (*www.leadership-studies.com/lsw/definitions.htm, accessed 22 Oct 2010*)

7   Bennis, W. (1989) *On Becoming a Leader*, Cambridge, Perseus Publishing

8   Luthans, F. (2005) *Organizational Behavior*, 10th edition, New York, McGraw-Hill, pp. 547

9   Covey, R. Stephen (1989) *The Seven Habits of Highly Effective People*, London, Simon & Schuster Ltd, pp-101

10 www.leadership501.com/leadership-quotes (accessed 12 March 2011)

11 www.futurevisions.org/ldr_mgr.htm (accessed 20 Apr 2011)

12 Ibid

13   Ibid

14   Sutton (2010) *True Leaders are also Managers*, Harvard Business Review article of August 2010 (Extracted from MBA Depot at http://www.mbadepot.com/newsletters accessed on 5 Nov 2010)

15   Adair, J. (2003) *Not Bosses but Leaders*, 3rd edition, New Delhi, Kogan Page, pp 53-54

16   Adair, J. (2005) *How to grow Leaders*, London, Kogan Page, pp.43-44

17   Burns, J. McGregor (1978) *Leadership*. New York, Harper & Row, pp-51

18   Ibid

19   Northouse, P. G. (2010) *Leadership: Theory and Practice*, 5th edition, California, Sage Publications, pp-19

20   U.S. Army 23 Traits of Character *at www.nwlink.com/~donclark/leader/leadchr.html* (accessed 25 Oct 2010)

21   Maxwell, John C. (1999) *The 21 Indispensable Qualities of a Leader*, Tennessee (USA), Thomson Nelson Publishers

22   Daft, R. L. (2008) *The Leadership Experience*, 4th edition, USA, Thomson South-Western, pp-64

23   Bose, C. (2002) *Principles of Management and Administration*, New Delhi, Prentice Hall, pp-168

24   Luthans, F. (2005) *Organizational Behavior,* 10th edition, New York, McGraw-Hill, pp. 555-558 & 584

25   Hollyforde & Whiddett (2005) *The Motivation Handbook*, Mumbai, Jaico Publishing House, pp-103

26   Luthans, F. (2005) *Organizational Behavior*, 10th edition, New York, McGraw-Hill, pp. 552-555

27   Adair, J. (2003) *Not Bosses but Leaders*, 3rd edition, New Delhi, Kogan Page, pp 15-17

28   Iftikhar Ahmed (2011) *Principles of Business War*, (Online), Available: http://www.mbadepot.com/content/17690/

29 Kotler, P. (2003) *Marketing Management*, 11th edition, New Jersey, Education Inc, pp.265-266

30 en.wikipedia.org/wiki/For_Want_of_a_Nail_(proverb) (accessed 15 March 2011)

31 Hazrat Ali's famous epistle to Malik Ashtar, Governor of Egypt, translated from Arabic by Rasheed Turabi, reprinted by Pakistan Navy Book Club, Islamabad

32 Munter, M. (1987) *Business Communication; Strategy and Skill*, New Jersey, Prentice Hall Inc, pp 40-43

33 Munter, M. (1987) *Business Communication; Strategy and Skill*, New Jersey, Prentice Hall Inc, pp 9

34 Bassi, Laurie quoted in http://www.nwlink.com/~donclark/hrd/trainsta.html (accessed 23 July 2010)

35 Hensey, M. (2001) *Collective Excellence: Building Effective Teams*, 2nd edition, USA, ASCE Press, pp-6

36 Kohn and O'Connell (2008) Six Habits of Highly Effective Teams, Easy Read Large Edition, US, Read How You Want (RHYW) at *books.google.com.pk (accessed 12 November 2010)*

37 Canning, Tuchinsky and Campbell (2005) *Building Effective Teams*, Chicago, Dearborn Trade Publishing, pp-2

38 http://www.amsc.belvoir.army.mil/AMSC_Perspectives_Leadership.pdf (accessed 20 Apr 2011)

39 Maslow, A.H. (1954) *Motivation and Personality*, 2nd Edition. New York, Harper & Row, pp. 35-47

40 McClelland, D.C. (1961) *The Achieving Society*. Princeton, D Van Nostrand Company, Inc

41 *Ibid*, pp.91-93

42 Steers & Porter (1987) Motivation and Work Behaviour, 4th edition, Singapore, McGraw-Hill, pp. 93

43 Hollyforde & Whiddett (2005) *The Motivation Handbook*. Mumbai, Jaico Publishing House, pp.76-82

44   Hackman, J.R. and Oldham, G.R. (1976) 'Motivation through the design of work: a test of a theory'. *Organizational Behavior and Human Performance,* Vol. 16. pp. 250-279

45   Ford, Donald J. (1999) *Bottom-Line Training.* Texas, Gulf Publishing Company, pp. 13)

46   Luthans, F. (2005) *Organizational Behavior,* 10th edition, New York, McGraw-Hill, pp. 555-557

47   Robbins and Coulter (2007) *Management,* 9th edition, India, Dorling Kindersley, pp.496

48   Hazrat Ali's famous epistle to Malik Ashtar, Governor of Egypt, translated from Arabic by Rasheed Turabi, reprinted by Pakistan Navy Book Club, Islamabad